MOTHER SHIPTON:
THE MISSING PROPHECIES

Anthony Austin

MOTHER SHIPTON: THE MISSING PROPHECIES

Copyright © Anthony Austin 2012

ISBN: 978-178035-518-4

First edition published by Black Rabbit Press 2003

The right of Anthony Austin to be identified as the author of this work has
been asserted by him in accordance with the Copyright, Designs and
Patents Act 1988 and any subsequent amendments thereto.

A catalogue record for this book is available from the British Library

An environmentally friendly book printed and bound in England by
www.printondemand-worldwide.com

Mixed Sources
Product group from well-managed
forests, and other controlled sources
www.fsc.org Cert no. TT-COC-002641
© 1996 Forest Stewardship Council
FSC

PEFC Certified
This product is
from sustainably
managed forests
and controlled
sources
PEFC
PEFC/16-33-415
www.pefc.org

This book is made entirely of chain-of-custody materials

Other works by the authors –

'Return to Mars'
Crowley and Pollock, Magistra 1989
and Black Rabbit Press, 2003.

'The New Life Prophecies of Frances Yule'
        Ed. Venestus
Destiny Publications NZ, 1982.

'The Dragon's Tail'
Austin and Crowley, IllumiNet 2000.

'The Sand Whales of Mars'
Austin and Mcleod,
Black Rabbit Press, 2001.

'Draco: The Tenth Planet'
Austin and Crowley,
with Christopher Mundy
Black Rabbit Press, 2003.

'Valley of Eden'
Austin
Black Rabbit Press, 2008.

'Keepers of the Black Stone'
Austin
Black Rabbit Press, 2011.

Our sincere thanks to

All who contributed to this work including
Miss Frances Yule, Anthony B Austin,
David Townsend, Martin Leo, John O'Hara,
Michelle Crossin, Piachi Diddicoy, Jill Startup,
and the Google Search Engine.

MOTHER SHIPTON:
THE MISSING PROPHECIES

Contents:

MOTHER SHIPTON:
THE MISSING PROPHECIES

PREFACE

A short history -

Work on this book commenced in late 1980 with the collation of numerous prophecies and other material given by Miss Frances Yule to Anthony Austin in Ponsonby, Auckland, New Zealand. Frances Yule is better known as Fran or Franji, born a Scorpio in Australia although she spent a quarter century in New Zealand before returning to her homeland. There is a website where more detail is given, including some photographs, showing that Miss Yule is a devotee of Meher Baba, an Indian whose country she recently visited. Naturally, many of Miss Yule's predictions concern the southern hemisphere and are reflected in the verses of Anthony Austin although their predictions do not always coincide.

Austin travelled to Australia from New Zealand in 1981 where he typed out much of Yule's work, publishing this as a booklet entitled *The New Life Prophecies of Frances Yule* in South Australia in 1982, as a run of 500 copies. Very few of these are in existence as at least half were destroyed in Victoria in the late '80s, and an ISBN was beyond Austin's ken. Austin returned from Australia to England in 1990 and still resides in this country of his birth, living in West Sussex only a few miles from the sea.

Austin set up Black Rabbit Press in 2001 to publish works on the planet Mars, commencing with *The Sand Whales of Mars* which was written in conjunction with Paul McLeod, then of Sydney, Australia, whose work can be found on the Net at various sites in the form of pictures of anomalous objects seen on the surface of Mars.

While still in Australia, Austin was living in the bush near Dunolly in the State of Victoria, where he was a gold-miner. Having little to do in late 1990, Austin decided to rewrite the prophecies of Frances Yule, but this soon included predictions of his own that had nothing to do with Yule's insights, amounting to 365 four-line verses originally named 'Third Millennium'. This was typed on a portable typewriter in 1990 in a steady run of sessions over a couple of months, ending before Christmas, when Austin returned to the UK in consideration of the fact that his father had cancer, from which he subsequently recovered, to the amazement of his doctors.

Austin wrote ten more verses in two sets in 1996 and 2002, making 375 in all, with the half-formed intention of reaching one thousand verses, which was never accomplished. Following Nostradamus, the verses were arranged in 'centuries' of which the fourth was incomplete.

There are at least two copies of Third Millennium in existence, dating from 1992, of which one is in Austin's possession and another was sent to Prince Charles, both having the same verse numbers as appear in this, the second edition. The only changes between 1990 and 2003 were the addition of the last ten verses and numerous explanations in italics, together with a few cartoons and charts.

These explanations have been added to for the second edition in those cases where prophecies were fulfilled between 2003 and 2012, and some where failures are identified. To those who expect one hundred per cent accuracy, this has never been achieved by any prophet, and the best that will be done is about 60 to 70 per cent. It is most unusual for exact dating to be achieved for, as Yule said, *"Looking into the future is like battling a mighty gale that blows the harder the further the seer looks."* Usually, the seer will only be accurate one or two years into the future, and it is unwise to give exact dates although this can be done. Taking a lesson from the past, Yule's dated prophecies from 1981 to 2036 have been deleted, while those dates that remain should be treated with caution. It is better to say 'When this happens – then that will happen', as for instance, in IV:53 where the clean-up after 9/11 is described in terms of the rule of New York Mayor Rudi Giuliani. Here I apologise for spelling mistakes which were not deliberate although to be found here and there.

The question as to the accuracy of any particular prediction cannot be determined at a later date because accuracy depends on the degree to which the seer was 'switched on' or in the proper frame of mind. While the author could concoct another 375 prophecies, he has currently no intention of doing so.

If it should be asked: why is this book entitled *The Missing Prophecies*, it should be explained that there are numerous versions of Mother Shipton's prophecies which are all forgeries, including those by Robert Head and Charles Hindley, as well as the so-called 'Nexus' prophecies as printed by Nexus magazine of Queensland between 1993 and 1995, attributed to

Mother Shipton but very probably from the hand of Frances Yule, who has never denied nor confirmed authorship. These Nexus prophecies can be found repeated on the Net and are reproduced here with the addition of verse numbers not found elsewhere. This was done for convenience so as to break up the text into obvious portions of varying length as seemed appropriate. Frances Yule did not (or could not) type and the mythology of the Nexus verses includes a note that they were delivered to the Editor of Nexus in hand-written form. Nexus subsequently refused to publish prophecy although it featured in their earlier editions. Once bitten....

It is well known that the last dated verse attributed to the 19th century forger Charles Hindley is that which says, *"The World to an end will come in 1881."* However, there are additional verses which are attributed to Hindley or Shipton which are also forgeries, such as those that describe modern inventions like the combine harvester:

> *"A roaring monster with man atop*
> *doth seem to eat the verdant crop"*

When it is agreed that the last verse attributed to Charles Hindley or his imitators describes the conditions of World War II, about 1945, then there is a considerable gap before we reach verse 18 (amounting to something between 50 and 170 years) and the arrival of a fiery dragon. This 'dragon' is thought to be Hercolobus or Nibiru, to use two of many names, otherwise Planet X or the tenth planet of the Solar System. It is described several times in these prophecies as a 'Dragon', hence the author's book entitled *The Dragon's Tail*. If it is assumed, as stated, that the Dragon will arrive close to our Earth in the year 2115, then 170 years would go by between 1945 and 2115, hence the statement that up to 170 years are missing from the Nexus prophecies.

On the other hand, if the Dragon should appear in 2012, as per the Mayan prophecies, then about 67 years would be missing. It is this author's opinion that the Mayan prophecies are in fact a recitation of ancient history combined with calendrical assumptions that are not our province. Moreover, a portion of the Mayan prophecies is actually illegible, using the most often seen codex, of which there are very few due to the idiocy of Catholic priests in South and Central America in centuries past who destroyed what they could not understand.

To return to the history of this volume, in 2011 the advertised price of a second-hand copy reached £297 on Amazon (from an American bookseller) because Black Rabbit Press had taken it out of print. This was done because of the need for revision of the text. Anyone requiring a copy of the original (i.e. *Third Millennium*) can have one, hand produced, for the same money, i.e. £297.

As for details of Mother Shipton, it is suggested that the reader obtain one of the several recent books that have appeared since 2003, when our text was originally published, and that you make of these what you will. It is not desired to reproduce any of Mother Shipton's doubtful history here, or should we say, legendary fiction. This all-too-human penchant for forgery and fiction for commercial gain was added to but not originated by the Shipton forgers, Robert Head and Charles Hindley, and compounded by a mysterious woman in association with the Nexus magazine, thought by this author to have been Miss Frances Yule.

I conclude with the observation that no prophet has any honour in his own country, and probably none until he/she is dead. It is also confirmed that James Randi did not accept the challenge issued in this volume nor pay any money for proof that psychic power exists. One might equally well challenge him to prove that it does not.

I should also add that writing and publishing are both games for fools in that there are too many books in this world, not to mention too many computers and gee-whizz devices invented to distract us from thinking, but I do not advocate the burning of any more libraries. When we destroy our past, we have no key to the future. Soon, all we will be left with is the *Da Vinci Code* and *Harry Potter*.

For those who *still* do not believe in the power of prophecy to get things right *sometimes*, we refer you to III:93 where the Mississippi was forecast to crest on April 23, which it did in 2001 at Davenport, USA.

October 2012   Anthony Austin

The Shipton / Hindley Prophecies

1. A carriage without horse will go
   Disaster fill the world with woe.
   In London, Primrose Hill shall be
   In centre hold a Bishop's See.

2. Around the world men's thoughts will fly
   Quick as the twinkling of an eye.
   And water shall great wonders do
   How strange. And yet it shall come true.

3. Through towering hills proud men shall ride
   No horse or ass move by his side.
   Beneath the water, men shall walk
   Shall ride, shall sleep, shall even talk
   And in the air men shall be seen
   In white and black and even green.

4. A great man then, shall come and go
   For prophecy declares it so.

5. In water, iron then shall float
   As easy as a wooden boat.
   Gold shall be seen in stream and stone
   In land that is yet unknown.

6. And England shall admit a Jew
   You think this strange, but it is true.
   The jew that once was held in scorn
   Shall of a Christian then be born.

7. A house of glass shall come to pass
   In England. But alas, alas
   A war will follow with the work
   Where dwells the Pagan and the Turk.

8   These states will lock in fiercest strife
     And seek to take each other's life.
     When north shall thus divide the south
     And Eagle build in Lion's mouth
     Then tax and blood and cruel war
     Shall come to every humble door.

9   Three times shall lovely sunny France
     Be led to play a bloody dance
     Before the people shall be free
     Three tyrant rulers shall she see.

10   Three rulers in succession be
     Each springs from different dynasty.
     Then when the fiercest strife is done
     England and France shall be as one.

11   The British olive shall next then twine
     In marriage with a German vine.
     Men walk beneath and over streams
     Fulfilled shall be their wondrous dreams.

12   For in those wondrous far-off days
     The women shall adopt a craze
     To dress like men, and trousers wear
     And to cut off their locks of hair.
     They'll ride astride with brazen brow
     As witches do on broomstick now.

13   And roaring monsters with man atop
     Does seem to eat the verdant crop
     And men shall fly as birds do now
     And give away the horse and plough.

14   There'll be a sign for all to see
     Be sure that it will certain be.
     Then love shall die and marriage cease
     And nations wane as babes decrease.

15   And wives shall fondle cats and dogs
     And men live much the same as hogs.

16   In nineteen hundred and twenty six
Build houses light of straw and sticks.
For then shall mighty wars be planned
And fire and sword shall sweep the land.

17   When pictures seem alive with movements free
When boats like fishes swim beneath the sea
When men like birds shall scour the sky
Then half the world, deep drenched in blood shall die.

18   For those who live the century through
In fear and trembling this shall do.
Flee to the mountains and the dens
To bog and forest and wild fens.

19   For storms will rage and oceans roar
When Gabriel stands on sea and shore
And as he blows his wondrous horn
Old worlds die and new be born.

20   A fiery Dragon will cross the sky
Six times before this Earth shall die
Mankind will tremble and frightened be
For the sixth heralds in this prophecy.

21   For seven days and seven nights
Man will watch this awesome sight.
The tides will rise beyond their ken
To bite away the shores, and then
The mountains will begin to roar
And earthquakes split the plain to shore.

22   And flooding waters, rushing in
Will flood the lands with such a din
That mankind cowers in muddy fen
And snarls about his fellow men.

23   He bares his teeth and fights and kills
And secrets food in secret hills
And ugly in his fear, he lies
To kill marauders, thieves and spies.

24   Man flees in terror from the floods
And kills, and rapes and lies in blood
And spilling blood by mankind's hands
Will stain and bitter many lands.

25   And when the Dragon's tail is gone
Man forgets, and smiles, and carries on
To apply himself—too late, too late
For mankind has earned deserved fate.

26   His masked smile, his false grandeur
Will serve the Gods their anger stir.
And they will send the Dragon back
To light the sky—his tail will crack
Upon the Earth and rend the Earth
And man shall flee, King, Lord, and serf.

27   But slowly they are routed out
To seek diminishing water spout
And men will die of thirst before
The oceans rise to mount the shore.
And lands will crack and rend anew
You think it strange. It will come true.

28   And in some far-off distant land
Some men—oh such a tiny band
Will have to leave their solid mount
And span the Earth, those few to count.

29   Who survives this [unreadable] and then
Begin the human race again.
But not on land already there
But on ocean beds, stark, dry and bare.

30   Not every soul on Earth will die
As the Dragon's tail goes sweeping by.
Not every land on Earth will sink
But these will wallow in stench and stink
Of rotting bodies of beast and man
Of vegetation crisped on land.

31   But the land that rises from the sea
       Will be dry and clean and soft and free
       Of mankind's dirt and therefore be
       The source of man's new dynasty.
       And those that live will ever fear
       The Dragon's tail for many year
       But time erases memory
       You think it strange. But it will be.

32   And before the race is built anew
       A silver serpent comes to view
       And spew out men of like unknown
       To mingle with the Earth now grown
       Cold from its heat, and these men can
       Enlighten the minds of future man
       To intermingle and show them how
       To live and love and thus endow
       The children with the second sight.
       A natural thing so that they might
       Grow graceful, humble, and when they do
       The Golden Age will start anew.

33   The Dragon's tail is but a sign
       For mankind's fall and man's decline.
       And before this prophecy is done
       I shall be burned at the stake, at one
       My body singed and my soul set free
       You think I utter blasphemy
       You're wrong. These things have come to me.
       This prophecy will come to be.

34   The signs will be there for all to read,
       When man shall do most heinous deed
       Man will ruin kinder lives,
       By taking them as to their wives.

35   And murder foul and brutal deed,
       When man will only think of greed.
       And man shall walk as if asleep,
       He does not look—he many not peep
       And iron men the tail shall do,
       And iron cart and carriage too.

36   The kings shall false promise make,
And talk just for talking's sake
And nations plan horrific war,
The like as never seen before
And taxes rise and lively down,
And nations wear perpetual frown.

37   Yet greater sign there be to see,
As man nears latter century.
Three sleeping mountains gather breath,
And spew out mud, and ice and death.
And earthquakes swallow town and town,
In lands as yet to me unknown.

38   And Christian one fights Christian two,
And nations sigh, yet nothing do
And yellow men great power gain,
From mighty bear with whom they've lain.

39   These mighty tyrants will fail to do,
They fail to split the world in two.
But from their acts a danger bred,
An ague, leaving many dead.

40   And physics find no remedy,
For this is worse than leprosy.
Oh many signs for all to see,
The truth of this true prophecy.

41   I know I go, I know I'm free
I know that this will come to be.
Secreted this, for this will be
Found by later dynasty.

42   A dairy maid, a bonny lass
Shall kick this tome as she does pass
And five generations she shall breed
Before one male child does learn to read.

43   This is then held year by year
Till an iron monster trembling fear
Eats parchment, words and quill and ink
And mankind is given time to think.

44 And only when this comes to be
    Will mankind read this prophecy
    But one man's sweet's another's bane
    So I shall not have burned in vain.

Spiral UFO seen in Russia, 2006
Verse 4:37

Eden Project, Cornwall, 2001
Verse 4:47

The following was printed at: http://rexresearch.com and is compared with the Nexus prophecies. (Numbers refer to MSHIP enumeration.)

"Carriages without horses shall go.	
And accidents fill the world with woe.	*compare (1) 'disaster'*
Around the world thoughts shall fly	
In the twinkling of an eye.	
Waters shall yet more wonders do	
How strange, yet shall be true.	
The world upside down shall be	
And gold be found at the root of tree.	*compare (5) root of tree missing in Nexus edn.*
Through the hills man shall ride	*compare (3) 'towering' an unnecessary addition*
And no horse be at his side.	
Underwater men shall walk.	
Shall ride, shall sleep, shall talk.	
In the air man shall be seen	
In white, in black, in green:	
Gold shall be found in mid stone	*compare (5) 'mid stone' and 'stream'*
In a land that's now unknown;	*compare 'yet' and 'now'. Australia, 1850s*
Fire and water shall wonders do,	*compare (2) where 'fire' is missing.*
England shall admit a Jew.	*compare (6) three lines missing here.*
Women will dress like man and trousers wear,	
And cut off all their locks of hair.	
They will ride astride with brazen brow.	*compare (12) where 'witches' deleted here.*
And love shall die, and marriage cease,	*chronologically inaccurate, late 20th century*
And nations wane and babes decrease,	
And wives shall fondle cats and dogs;	
And men shall live much like hogs,	
Just for food and lust.	*compare (15). This line has no rhyming couplet and does not scan*
When pictures look alive, with movements free,	*Victorian 'flip-books' and arcade machines.*
When ships, like fishes, swim beneath the sea,	*submarines. 19th c.*
When men, outstripping birds, can soar the sky,	*early 20th century?*
Then half the world, deep-drenched in blood, shall die,	*World War I*
The fiery year as soon as over,	*(1918) compare Nexus (17), (18),*
Peace shall then be as before,	*where this passage down to 'snow*

15

Plenty everywhere be found,
And men with swords shall plow the ground.

All England's sons that plow the land,
Shall be seen with book in hand.
Learning shall so ebb and flow,
The poor shall most wisdom know.
And water wind where corn doth grow;
Great houses stand in farflung vale,
All covered o'er with snow and hail.
Taxes for blood and war
Shall come to every door.
And state and state in fierce strife
Will seek after each other's life.
But when the North shall divide the South,
An Eagle shall build in the Lion's mouth.
In London Primrose Hill shall be,
Its centre hold a Bishop's See.
Three times shall lovely France
Be led to play a bloody dance;
Before the people shall be free,
Three tyrant rulers shall she see;
Three times the people's hope is gone,

Three rulers in succession, be ....
Each sprung from different dynasty.
Then, when the fiercest fight is done,
England and France shall be as one.
The British olive next shall entwine
In marriage with the German vine
The Jew that once was held in scorn
Shall of a Christian be born.
A house of glass shall come to pass
In England --- but alas! Alas!
A war will follow with the work
Where dwells the Pagan and the Turk.
The gods will send the Dragon back
To light the sky his tail will crack
Upon the Earth and rend the Earth
And man shall flee, King, Lord and serf."

and hail' is missing. Dated to post WWI when universal State Education in the UK became compulsory and horses were still used for ploughing but aircraft had been invented and used in warfare.
compare (13) re. 'horse and plough' where internal combustion combine harvesters are described, post WWII Possibly 1930s

compare (8) Alteration of line order
compare (1) Alteration of verse order

compare (10) this line is missing in Nexus

compare (6) alteration of verse order

compare (7) alteration of verse order

End of Hindley Prophecies
compare Nexus 26!! And Yule

16

THIRD MILLENNIUM

'*SI KHOKHAIMO MAY PACHIVALO
SAR O CHACHIMO*'

There are lies more believable than truth

Trad Romany

Fukushima disaster and
Consequences, 2010
Verse 4:5

THIRD MILLENNIUM

CHRONOLOGY

1990 - 2005	Rise of the New World Order
2006 - 2034	Age of the Prophets
2025 - 2042	Years of the Floods
2063 - 2115	World Council
2115 - 2190	First Great Sign and Consequences
2200 - 2500	Dark Age, or Little Ice Age
2500 - 2506	Peace
2506 - 2600	The Five Great Asian Wars
2600 - 2800	Age of the Nomads
2803 - 2856	The New Beast
2856 - 2862	The New Solar System
2990 - 2995	Recolonisation of the Moon
2995 - 3000	The Psychic Wars
3001 - 3034	Preparation for Exodus
3007 - 3033	Second Great Sign and Consequences
3034 - 3035	Exodus
4032 - 4061	Silver Age begins
7700	Bronze Age begins

note: At present, we live in the Age of Iron. This will be followed by the Ages of Gold, Silver, and Bronze (or copper) followed by another Age of Iron.

CENTURY I

CENTURY I

1   An eerie lull in affairs of Mankind
    as Europe knits together   *Channel tunnel breakthrough*
    The Czechs shall turn the East behind   *Czech free of the USSR*
    as England turns to another   *Thatcher dismissed Nov 1990*

2   Clouds now gather in minds of men   *Post Gulf war*
    The Chinese look for new conquests   *China claims China Sea*
    Leaders, uneasy, topple when   *About 15 world leaders fell*
    brave pride rises in Frenchmen's breasts   *French Referendum Sep 1992*

3   Riots, oppressions trouble the world   *Fall of Yugoslavia*
    Two sons would usurp their father   *Bush and Cheney*
    Four new flags in Africa unfurled
    Australia, Europe, fight together   *Bosnia-Herzgovina 1992 - 3*

4   There is no patience in his way   *George F Bush and American*
    No peaceful passive content   *conflicts*
    waiving instant reaction of anger
    annoyance, then aggression sent   *Gulf War 1, August 1990*

5   The sword has struck full seven times
    and of the six, you have long wondered
    Wrapt in your euphoric liberty
    Inevitable fog, the mind enshrouded

6   Two institutions, worlds, nations
    once torn apart but now in train
    are made of tin and left in rain   *Road to Basra?*
    to rust away, a bloody red stain

7   Ramigny of Italy, but not in his land   *Mario Monti, PM, 2011-13*
    near Christmas sees a sensation
    Guided by an experienced hand
    Two years service, a greater nation

8   The sons, by cunning, will attain high places *George W. Bush and*
    The rise of the Beast advances   *vice-pres Cheyne*
    And starting among the northern races
    a false New Order entrances   *War against terrorism*

CENTURY I

9   Attempting to conquer all the globe   *Osama bin Laden*
    the younger knows naught but evil
    Lust and greed never earned such robe
    The plotting is that of the Devil   *Al Qaeda*

10   The pair, each thought to be Elijah
    Apart, yet linked, predict the future
    Churches quake in reborn terror   *Red heifer born and Wailing*
    Some decipher a new Messiah   *Wall weeps, Israel. 2001 -02*

11   The fiery pit and the flying ash
    will destroy all trace of green
    for those who live on caldera's edge
    mud and reed where Kaitawo was seen   *Anagram*

12   Gold in the dawnlight, the comet then
    so brilliant and pure arising
    Viewed by the boy-king Tutankhamen
    three times in its returning

13   The omens read, the world in confusion   *Gothenburg 'Elite' conference*
    Stockholm requires double or nothing   *June 2001*
    Fanatics insist that they see everything
    Occultists win by the global fusion

14   Science strives against pollution
    A false prophet soon is murdered
    Africa dying through retribution   *Murder and AIDS rates soar*
    The Prophet's word is then recorded

15   The Prophet elucidates and heals
    on the borders of Nepal
    Known to few, not on the news reels
     A new sign among celestial halls

16   Frisco reels, Salt Lake in full cry
    Battle dress of brown and red
    The homeless hungry negro will try
    The East Coast victors, blood will shed

CENTURY I

17 The truce is signed while Man still thinks
    the corner is turned and all is rosy
    A New Age begins amidst filth and stinks
    The air and sea are both grey and hazy

18 He who was on February eighth born
    will be better then in August known
    A public holiday month decreed
    when the sword-like comet has flown

19 Unpredictable, laughing, gay
    Incisive, ugly, amid a new plague
    Church and State in disarray
    mend their fences, grim intrigue

20 Australia seals her every border
    Cross and Sword meet overhead
    Racial strife, strange fruit, disorder
    Thousands seen at the temple dead

21 Mercury in front and Venus behind
    the light shall outshine the light
    arresting the world in way and mind
    for seven times day and night

22 His almighty gaze, a silent breath
    the goats cannot comprehend
    the soulless ones condemned to death
    a beginning and seven to end

23 The ignorant ones fall on the ground
    rejecting the visage so marred
     no saving grace in him is found
    and so find themselves debarred

24 The religious ones seek gifts of mercy
    salvation for the self righteous
    each hears and sees quite differently
    and thus comes disorder in each house

CENTURY I

25   Twenty three years before the turn
      the Chosen One and Satan both
      each the Crown will try to earn
      in the same year returning to Earth

26   Six, the Smiling Prophet,
      to the King of Kings will wend
      Late October, in dust and heat
      an old acknowledged friend

27   They will listen to this Chosen One
      in the dawning of the Sun
      voices praise, millions run,
      short the time till the work is done

28   Seven, and the great march then begins
      the soulless war with the saved
      black plague strikes, six years wins
      Asia with dead ones shall be paved

29   Armageddon two years shall last
      mad dogs in shattered Europe tear
      China shall not withstand the blast
      February, New Guinea her cross will bear

30   Nine, and the Cock shall finally fall
      neutral now stands the Bear
      China's patriots heed their call
      the Eagle cannot herself repair

31   The United Nations power is spent
      Peace enforced by the German Hall
      North Africa heads the New World Church
      Past fifty, the Negro shall install

32   Seven, and the Prophet southwards has gone
      Welcome by the land of the russet rock
      To write and teach in the hall of the don
      By pole and Yssa they will take stock   *anagram*

CENTURY I

33   Seven to eleven the great East reels   *failed*
Mongolia, China, loss in Cambodia
the new road cut, Bear hears appeals
Jewish accord with the new Master

34   New City, new light, established in Aza
near the dead city resurrected
five miles north, the house of treasure
the pillar there shall be erected

35   They build of stone of rose and white
throne and house he does not require
walls that gleam in sun as gold light
words graven there he does not desire

36   Twelve, and the madness not yet over
brown dress, red crosses, together seen
white kills white in south hemisphere
waving flags of white and green

37   The fascist rise in Berlin is stopped
thirteen the Prophet gives his orders
for farming now the world will opt
to feed nine billion across the borders

38   Fourteen, and the wastelands are explored
Indian pacifist Joseph dies
Parisian gay life no longer adored
thirteen shot as foreign spies

39   A warmer world, but the die is cast
the waters rise and the crops grow fast
Skirmishes, Jordan, Israeli boast
millions panic beside each coast

40   Twenty and one sees a reborn Ark
but the Prophet never is heard
geysers, volcanoes, the Age grows dark
at the supposed failure of his word

CENTURY I

41   Error is laid at science's door
       for the technofix has failed
       to cure the evils that science caused
       thousands murdered, none are jailed

42   Twenty and two the prophets arise
       speaking then of a new Dark Age
       thousands of cults, miniscule size
       black children killed, fits of rage

43   Four, the cults with long knives and guns
       terrorise those who do not believe
       India says through her holy ones
       she will last forever while they live

44   Five to nine brings Joe Vershmeer
       and the oceans are rising still
       the Devil's People crucify this seer
       by damnation, the Beast, and Hell

45   Thirty, to ancient time worn stones
       the Prophet and the few, seclusion
       there he will rest his weary bones
       newly armed, they seek his destruction

46   The teachers then dissolve and hide
       no-one hears the truth if spoken
       chaos to the north, the south abides
       all covenants, laws, now are broken

47   Ajita Hari dies, reincarnation
       resurrecting an ancient myth
       mourning, for some a celebration
       and madness begins on Earth herewith

48   Thirty four, twelve years, madness apace
       world government aims for the Moon
       trying to contact the Masters of Space
       cramped chiefs and military goons

CENTURY I

49   Ten years old Neptune extends his domain
roaring waves, savants wise words
they throw the babies in wind and rain
competing on high with goats and birds

50   Forty, land sinks, armadas of boats
Hari ignored, the new god is Triton
sacrifice, murder, madness by rote
they seek new lands they can live on

51   Whirlpools, tension, death by waters
new deserts, swamps, remind of Atlantis
volcanos, quakes, high new geysers
Aza now green, where the new lake is

52   Two and forty, old outnumber the young
grain in plenty, no money to buy it
rotted fish where there is no dung
they reorganize, never will quit

53   Those of the West who would rule the world
the four year war, flames, destruction
selfishness, terror, desperation
reduces the World near a hundred million

54   Seven and forty, peace, plagues of fish
resurgence of dolphins and whales
in Vermont is found the depressing cache
the supply of most metals now fails

55   Papers, tapes, the nightmare collection
the effluvia of the great rampant Beast
the underground cult destroyed a nation
two years before all shall stand aghast

56   Rebuilding the world, politics extinct
the Wolf will scrounge her friends anew
The Isles, and those who border the Strait
under black banners, to fight the blue

CENTURY I

57   Two years on and the hordes beaten back
the old grey King will relent
the dishes done, the cables slack
the force of Asia then is spent

58   In Aza then two tongues are spoken
for new masters the poor white labours
the new faith then it is awoken
through envy life loses its savour

59   Fifty three and the new reincarnation
Aza potters along, accepting the hordes
word of mouth throughout the nation
farming not factory owned by new lords

60   Four and the new man makes an appearance
the small fast craft are all the rage
peace at all costs is the nation's stance
aircraft have mostly left the stage

61   The weapons are gathered by strong big Joe
sixty two the Emperor of Aza
barter for food, a meal if you hoe
from Coon' the Jew, usurping another   *Coonabarrabran*

62   The faultline moved, half south half north
where forty years they once had wandered
at first they carry their world to the south
invited, pride, refusal, accepted

63   The abyss on the East, bones a-burning
the flooding sea to the west
chastened Arabs, to desert a-turning
Africa harrowed, to chaos at best

64   Credit cards become antiques
money consigned to the flames
psychic people not seen as freaks
none of the bankers still remains

CENTURY I

65   Germany has not risen again
except in her great economy
by storing away, before the rain
by foresight, far from apathy

66   Aza claims all economic power
in the face of her northern rival
Big Joe would now go on much further
conference proposed and new trial

67   The powerful psychics look on with dread
foreseeing a world situation
where all will have to give gold for bread
and money enslave the nation

68   The missives sent, convene World Council
Five, Joe answers, Friends of the Earth
shall control all trade, cure all ill
new krona chips, of them no dearth

69   Chaos once again in sixty six
the red put high and the white is low
the principle of the old unionists
company 'gainst company strikes a blow

70   T & W begging, seek a parley
bringing threats from old Big Joe
the army destroys the grain & barley
when winter brings an early snow

71   Seventy four and the eerie message
heard again by every ear
lights in heaven make frequent passage
confusion, panic, death by fear

72   Silent on the sacred plain
once stood the mystic gate
in ninety one is set in train
the key to Mankind's fate

CENTURY I

73   By ninety eight the slow precession
     will draw new lines upon the Globe
     astrology tries to fix a new heaven
     science charts changes in magnetic lobe

74   One hundred and four, power has shifted
     sand now green, and green into sand
     the Council through its options sifted
     decides to abandon the African Rand

75   Six years teams chart rises and fall
     sailing through uncharted oceans
     assessing black mud and volcanic pall
     to heal Earth brewing strange potions

76   Eighteen, the Prophet, score off a century
     a reincarnation of the great Gimel
     revered, obeyed, is buried in Albury
     appointing a new three to rule well

77   The consequence of the Great Sign   *Recent calculation suggests 2115*
     will leave but eighty four million   *Tenth planet*
     Comet Tut swoops in twenty nine
     They will never count up to a billion

78   Stunned into silence, abandoning God
     hope cut short, in total surprise
     but still wearily ploughing the sod
     they thought the predictions were lies

79   Reason had taught that Man rules the Earth
     and the Book that he had dominion
     experience taught that his Lord, Blind Chance
     would deliver the final opinion

80   To a hundred and ninety the gloom will last
     a new Dark Age and tyrants and wars
     three hundred years, chaos holds them fast
     from end of the Council and laws

CENTURY I

81   Volcanic islands all shall sink
       explode or belch out lava
       New Zealand then goes to the brink
       the contagion will last a millennia

82   The island race which copied the West
       is shaken from end to end
       all must slide into the dark sea
       when they find that rocks upwards bend

83   Europe a hundred nations, not ten
       land of sea and mountain tops
       Germany rises but falls only when
       the rats shall leave nothing of crops

'Subsidiary', the division of Europe into 100 'Cantons' - the cornerstone of European 'integration'

84   Cape Horn a place of roaring water
       but never a sign there of ice
       to Arctic goes the West of America
       with a cargo of black rats and mice

error: brown rats

85   The dark skinned races of the Pacific
       returning from far distant shore
       relearning the arts of long navigation
       they will claim a million times more

86   The wilderness of North America
       melting tundra nearer the Pole
       the red and black ones then will claim her
       shaken, cratered, and without a goal

87   England in tilting, slowly sunken
       will lose of land up to a third
       and after the long black rain has fallen
       Scotland now reefs of the deer and bird

88   Old Dublin shall deepen her harbour
       when the Isles become so wet
       that grass will then grow much higher
       They will cancel the ancient debt

Record rainfall in the UK Sept – Dec 2000. In Feb 2001 it was proposed that the debt of 20 nations be cancelled. Simultaneous Foot & Mouth meant that grass was not eaten

CENTURY I

89 He who would lay with the maid of Derry
  will fight with his seven brothers
  where plunder stored of wreck of Skerry
  the owners will fight with the robbers

90 China will fight the Hahan States
  with the giant guns, not atomic
  uranium shall not decide their fates
  upper waters shall make them more sick

91 The five great wars last until six hundred
  fifteen million burned in the flame
  the northern Asians shall count their dead
  to India's eternal damned name

92 When tunnels are dug out from the shore
  the nomads will use a striped ass
  the book of the Twelve contains much lore
  explaining when and why of the lass

93 The Awakener's tome is found near the tomb
  he thought more of silence than words
  written by one, and placed in the room,
  the Book of New Life shall be hers

94 The barbaric few still roam and plunder
  they farm the land without fuel
  in the seventh, men, quite few in number
  shall prove the glassy power jewel   *Black Stone or Grail*

95 Late in the eighth, but not understood
  gravity found to be variable
  when new use is found for secret wood
  the cause is not discoverable

96 The days will then become much warmer
  through the swelling of the Sun
  Earth will find herself near Jupiter
  when three seven nine seven is done

CENTURY I

97   The eccentricity now brings seasons
hotter at first and then colder
the Moon departs for her good reasons
when the ninth is only half over

98   In fifty six they build a new Ark
resembling a floating low city
they could never walk from Africa
to Aza, and more is the pity

99   Slowly all Earth comes to the opinion
the hope is the Northern Cape
the Eagle shall fly upon new pinion
a great proud attempt to escape

100   The only untouched and livable land
for most of a thousand long years
industry, and the spiritual band
in Aza alone stands Man's heirs.

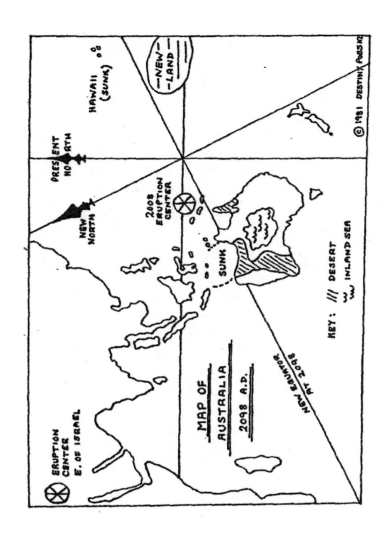

MAP OF AUSTRALIA 2098 A.D.

KEY: /// DESERT
www INLAND SEA

CENTURY II

CENTURY II

1   Answers lie in questions
     Sight depends not on eyes
     God gave us gifts neglected
     to all, not only the wise

2   When the planets are in disarray
     each a new orbit chosen
     closing the eighth, no time to pray
     before they are all fried or frozen

3   Deroath the Beast will reappear   *10th planet*
     Three thousand, four, and three
     he must be loosed a little while
     the dotted circle on the Tree

4   In eight hundred and fifty nine
     the outer two will meet
     night as dark as deep coal mine
     the second Moon will be fleet

5   Fireballs and meteors shower the sky
     three years in their arriving
     no-one will doubt the reason why
     the time was described in writing

6   Nine months later, about mid May
     all psychics will know of the hour
     the Deliverer turns up in the usual way
     aware in the leafy green bower

7   As though they had found the fountain of youth
     once near Bimini displayed
     they find the real truth of ancient sooth
     at a century not yet decayed

8   She whose number is thirty three
     will shoulder her load at nine
     on her orders awaits humanity
     solutions she shall re-define

CENTURY II

9   The Third Millennium less but nine
    the aged resurrect the past
    to reach the Moon base and the mine
    their colony shall not long last

10 Samantha office is held by four
    priestess teacher and adept all
    consecutively holding the floor
    each one year they shall install

11 Ninety two the threat perceived
    of the Aryan cult reborn
    in this the Hahan well deceived
    then met with steel and scorn

12 In ninety two the ship complete
    two thousand four hundred souls
    the abandoned dome shall be replete
    they burrow still further like moles

13 Few children born and fewer live
    again in three the Moon attracts
    the three their lives will shortly give
    from twenty, nothing more detracts

14 As long predicted weapons are banned
    when white magic fights with black
    the strange mind machines are manned
    and Korana begins to fight back

15 The eerie sights will imitate vision
    or sound at the adepts whim
    fire from the sky and dreadful dragons
    perplexed are both Lion and Lamb

16 The animal kingdom goes insane with Man
    the prayer of the wise is for peace
    because they have long abandoned God
    evil shall always increase

CENTURY II

17 From five to nine, before the turn
    her disciples Korana she gathers
    the worship of God shall then return
    but many shall worship their fathers

18 New land shall of a sudden rise
    where there was none before
    people then in new surprise
    of the future desire to learn more

19 The first of the eighth millennium
    they argue about the three zeros
    walls set up as in a dream
    when they deify horrible heros

20 The great ones terrify the least
    the motive is not described
    death outlawed before the feast
    the Kiwi has not still survived

21 The diagrams and the occult text
    thought to be two thousand old
    spells out the secret of the Gate
    to gather Man into the fold

22 Ru, the Vesica Pisces
    Ra, the name of the Sun
    Van the name by Hermes
    given to Ish which is Man

23 To conquer the light years which divide
    requiring a key not a hammer
    unites all men who now confide
    the question is when and not whether

24 Polarity balanced, the Gate radiates
    the Glory of God, Shekinah
    naked, no metal, the process dictates
    and conquers four axes, Selah

CENTURY II

25   Korana reveals the sacred book
       at Jenolan falsely concealed
       all humans then allowed to look
       at the secrets there revealed

26   The Most Great Peace of the Bab
       is realised in thirty one
       Mankind gathers all it may grab
       so to save all under the Sun

27   Thirty three the last whale dies
       an albino aged freak
       the soil it breeds no grubs or flies
       flying June-bugs whirr and squeak

28   Mosquitos and rats own a fading world
       both increased threefold in size
       ninety per cent at her feet are curled
       so few that Korana she cries

29   A year in passing, globe slowly turning
       to desert where snow never falls
       the ashes and lava from volcanos burning
       poisoned the hawks and the gulls

30   The Aquarian reality, long delayed
       is engineered by necessity
       Atalantis rising from the wave
       dry in its long declivity

31   Old Prydain sees the first device
       the wide red plain sees the third
       the second one shall be built in Yass
       on the island the fourth shall be gird

32   One year more, the choice then made
       to abandon the terminal hill
       to accept the future or it evade
       is an act of collective will

CENTURY II

33   Arrogant, tiny, puny one
demanding that the Universe
obey thy childish will
six thousand years didst thou curse

34   And thou art cursing still
Learn thy leaping ambition
will grind again six thousand
at the secret storing mill

35   Learn that the form of thinking life
nowhere else resembles Man
but five other races do abide
beyond thy ken or span

36   One thousand years, the Golden Age
closes in thirty and two
Zen the Way and the Man shall usher
in Sixty one the Silver Age new

37   The acres of bones lie bleached snow white
the buffalo, pale, ploughs the paddy
less than a hundred penguins delight
weary eyes in the thirty first century

38   Seven thousand seven hundred
has been reached by mortal vision
beyond, the future was never seen
time, space, mind, all conquered

39   The circling eye, channels and chasm   *Re-photographing the Face on*
Pavonis Ascraeus Olympica   *Mars*
both sides of the Face, reflex spasm
hidden, destroyed, out of terror

40   Out on the limit, the diverging two
murmuring, finding the tenth
found uncertain by the base crew
measuring orbit and length

CENTURY II

41   Jupiter in Pisces with Venus and Mars
the emerald victor, the tower burns
glasses smashed with long iron bars
the women gone, violated, by turns

42   Dry mud, long grass, seen at Rakiba   *Anagram*
after the measure is greater than eight
seen as if harrowed, for ever and ever,
through sickness, marakiba shall abate

43   The Spider is borne on a thread of breeze
one of a hundred, the King of Three
the Spider is found on the limbs of a tree
his web is spun of June intrigue

44   She who walked with the legs of a man   *Queen Elizabeth II, Maxwell,*
will see her realm broken and plucked   *Nadir, and others.*
the Eagle, a cuckoo in the land   *Late 80s, early 90s*
through poll and pillage dry sucked

45   The eldest old one shall die too early   *Prince Charles*
so that Wonder shall be placed in his stead
in his youth so handsome and burly
the first and last is found dead in bed

46   The widow so calm, later dressed in white
her children shall come to nothing
when the northern road is barriered tight
and the army ensures their returning

47   The ten nation Beast will lose more than three   *EU break up*
and dwindle away into eight   *End of Euro*
Bear, Wolf, Eagle, find great amity
Panda, Caribou, lose all hate

48   The subtle one of the Majlis
through diplomatic guile
will come to gather four crowns
but not their wealth in a while

CENTURY II

49   The Generals of Turkey sign a pact
      at night, peace still unbroken
      the common enemy would march due west
      declaration would never be spoken

50   The shade of Gessar Khan in eleven
      the peasant banners slowly stream
      from Agarthi the message it was given
      Balkh, they glance back at rosy gleam

51   At Karakoram and at Ubsa Nor
      Tibet, Narabanchi, Afghan
      Jain, Hindu, and Lamaite law
      set faces towards the western hand

52   Before the turn in a thunder storm rife   *Election of new Pope*
      the Frenchman shall be elected
      the founder chronicled Malachi's life
      to purify the Great Ones selected

53   Amid the wars pestilence, Sodom's sins
      after the Olive the White
      the Roman shall die when the Theatre falls
      too late, too little, his light

54   The brave small aged French commander
      shall think he sees the Evil One
      with tableware handy, sudden anger
      he does what he thinks should be done

55   The futile deed done at Pavia
      the Jew despairs of his life
      the banquet breaks up in disorder
      to West Coast death with his wife

56   The contests once seen in Roman days
      echoed in new Colosseum
      two sides move in opposite ways
      the pageant will end with Te Deum

CENTURY II

57   The signatures are seen by many
and those who at Warminster spy
the hoaxers bold think it so funny
but no Stendic sigil may lie

Increase in complexity of
crop circles post 80s

58   They say they will not believe at all
'til one lands on the White House lawn
the motive fear in Pentagon Hall
no defence, but in public, pure scorn

59   Someone else has claimed our Moon
mining for metals, making diamond
we steal away on little cat feet
knowing we come a poor second.

60   The silver glint of the reservoir
turns black when the angle is right
the cleared surround of every shore
stands out in the bright hard sunlight

Water on the Moon predicted

61   The number of saucer frights grows less
even fewer will be reported
They will never clear up our mess
because Mission Earth was aborted

62   Our place in Heaven shall be prepared
first Their coming then Their going
the destination at the start declared
beyond humankind's understanding

63   The trial is made in two times six
to give and to receive understanding
science will try to build with new bricks
confused, they fail to find meaning

ET contact

64   The answering of the questioner
who solves Christina's riddle
will take place in the theatre
in the last act at the middle

CENTURY II

65   In the city of silver black stone
choosing of sides and fierce hate
for one, a million long atone
commencing with a curved sword grate

66   When the last black raven croaks
by the White Tower of Lug's city
the barrage hidden by misty cloaks
and the music a tuneless ditty

67   The spirit of the little guide
turns the penitent priest to hope
but the murder by the open door
shall cheat the hangman's rope

68   For when the Shamrock and the Rose
unite against their common foe
through this false peace they suppose
the ending of trouble, war and woe.

69   From having gained the cowboy's ears   *Ronald Reagan, Gorbachev and*
to combat with Asia's horde   *the war against the Taliban*
Byrog counts to thirteen years   *1988 to 2001*
for wheat, new oil is stored

70   From the island munched down to the bones
born of island and German blood
to a land beside two ancient cones
recovers ten million for his people's good

71   Kasha's inheritance passed to Credo   *Kasha = anagram*
shattered pieces joined with handles
from Credo to Crowley they shall go
disbelief, then traces of scandals

72   Thou shalt not found graven on stone
sacred trust held by Impi warrior
told years before they shall atone
but the provenance hard to recover

CENTURY II

73 Geneva, Berne, through great disaster
will come to lose half of their gold
they shall appoint a great inspector
with the mountain of paper unsold

74 The mahogany ship is drilled clean through *Warrnambool*
and the date is sixteen seventy   *NSW – July '99*
a carrack manned by Portugese crew
at the close of the twentieth century

75 Out on the borders of old Yilgarnia
the soft ping on gold shall be heard
Lasseter's tale they shall discover
was more than a madman's last word

76 On eastern edge of wildflower State
at seventy ounces the ton
the last of Aza's discoveries great
two will die when the goldrush is done

77 After dropping to a single cent
the shares pushed up to a dollar
Longbush thieves silent on money spent
the Searcher shall to ARC deliver

78 Those who had pride in illegal wealth
but not through industry gained
their worthless pile is lost by stealth
slaves of the tax-man enchained

79 The Red Ones rejoice, old schisms healed
when Clement the Brune is elected
the secrets of Christ are never revealed
Gnostic Priory agreed when selected

80 A silver bird and carpet await
the second who escaped with his life
no rain nor wind, he knows his fate
nine miles, nine shots, nine days of strife

CENTURY II

81   All options closed, by the West deserted
the Pacific pair grow together
panic grows as the blossom fluttered
when the Basin Oil is the deliverer

82   Millions paid to high politicians
is traced to the New Hebrides
the dead pig's laughter echoes, missions   *'piggy' Muldoon*
of the Firm from the swinging sixties

83   The farmer, grey haired, from Taranaki
three friends they shall advise it
urgent message, death, compels destiny
when Colin has attained his limit

84   On the mountain road the seven decide
in peasant dress and bad disguise
the drop too sheer for wheels to ride
to capture soon through clever surmise

85   The idle dull princess of watches
who never gave birth to a child
obstinate, wilful, then she botches
her life with her brother so wild

86   When the target flies both low and fast
the old gun is close by his ear
the mother of three shall stand aghast
and follow within the year

87   Hold and log are bound by chains
fourteen, weather foul, ship unswerving
the crystal lost by waves and rain
is in Burmese hands by morning

88   He whose child was killed at Easter   *Col. Qaddafi and the*
for revenge almost two years abides   *Lockerbie disaster*
ships and men in the East to gather
to Malta then north, his small team rides

46

CENTURY II

89   Six years or seven, the rule like Poth   *Hun-Sen, Cambodia*
the terror then feared in renewal
relief shall come from the East and North
and never again such reversal

90   A swindler in food of Argentina
through reprieve shall quit the prison
after mourning, a day much brighter
a national figure on television

91   Blunt refusals of liberation
the migrants are turned into slaves
for most, rice paddy, desperation
for bricks, to dig their own graves

92   Where the army encircles Medina
the soldiers refuse their command
the angry Kurd will use a revolver
when the Sheikh shall refuse his demand

93   The two-faced French lady who cheated death
and found that her work was not done
through an orange cat shall meet a mad king
in a carriage, only aged twenty one

94   Rainbow chasing, the new laws are broken
the stunted crop like the last
the army arrives to ensure dispersion
and the children will die of the fast

95   Nostalgia for the redundant past
by Lac Leman turns to endeavour
loyal, patient, down to earth
the skilled prince bids them recover

96   Turkey's emmissary captured and held
abandoned then betrayed
the pipeline cut, they soon re-weld
dissatisfied, Iran to invade

CENTURY II

97   The Riyal breaks the generous treaty
Kuwait's general dies through a spanner
a token force from Italy not worthy
more money helps solve the dilemma

98   New course set by black south junta
before they have had white approval
thousands of feet of muddy brown water
will give them plenty of trouble

99   Women and children thrust to the front   *Saddam Hussein's war*
to face the gas and the cannon   *against the Kurds*
three thousand dead before the hunt
in the melee no mercy for anyone

100 At London awaiting the right time to act
the blast from Hendon is heard
the rust in the tank an unfortunate fact
rain and potash are quickly blurred

The Prophecy of Hermes Trismegistus

Do you not know, Asclepius, that Egypt is an image of heaven, or, to speak more exactly, in Egypt all the operations of the powers which rule and work in heaven have been transferred to earth below?

Nay, it should rather be said that the whole Kosmos dwells in this our land as in its sanctuary. And yet, since it is fitting that wise men should have knowledge of all events before they come to pass, you must not be left in ignorance of this: there will come a time when it will be seen that in vain have the Egyptians honoured the deity with heartfelt piety and assiduous service; and all our holy worship will be found bootless and ineffectual. For the gods will return from earth to heaven.

Egypt will be forsaken, and the land which was once the home of religion will be left desolate, bereft of the presence of its deities.

This land and region will be filled with foreigners; not only will men neglect the service of the gods, and Egypt will be occupied by Scythians or Indians or by some such race from the barbarian countries thereabout. In that day will our most holy land, this land of shrines and temples, be filled with funerals and corpses. To thee, most holy Nile, I cry, to thee I foretell that which shall be; swollen with torrents of blood, thou wilt rise to the level of thy banks, and thy sacred waves will be not only stained, but utterly fouled with gore.

Do you weep at this, Asclepius? There is worse to come; Egypt herself will have yet more to suffer; she will fall into a far more piteous plight, and will be infected with yet more, grievous plagues; and this land, which once was holy, a land which loved the gods, and wherein alone, in reward for her devotion, the gods deigned to sojourn upon earth, a land which was the teacher of mankind in holiness and piety, this land will go beyond all in cruel deeds. The dead will far outnumber the living: and the survivors will be known for Egyptians by their tongue alone, but in their actions they will seem to be men of another race.

O Egypt, Egypt, of thy religion nothing will remain but an empty tale, which thine own children in time to come will not believe; nothing will be left but graven words, and only the stones will tell of my piety. And in that day men will be weary of life, and they will cease to think the universe worthy of reverent wonder and of worship. And so religion, the greatest of all blessings, for there is nothing, nor has been, nor ever shall be, that can be deemed a greater boon, will be threatened with destruction; men will think it a burden, and will come to scorn it. They will no longer love this world around us, this incomparable work of God, this glorious structure which he has built, this sum of good made up of things of many diverse forms, this instrument whereby the will of God operates in that which be has made, ungrudgingly favouring man's welfare, this combination and accumulation of all the manifold things that can call! forth the veneration, praise, and love of the beholder. Darkness will be preferred to light, and death will be thought more profitable than life; no one will raise his eyes to heaven; the pious will be deemed insane, and the impious wise; the madman will be thought a brave man, and the wicked will be esteemed as good. As to the soul, and the belief that it is immortal by nature, or may hope to attain to immortality, as I have taught you, all this they will mock at, and will even persuade themselves that it is false. No word of reverence or piety, no utterance worthy of heaven and of the gods of heaven, will be heard or believed.

And so the gods will depart from mankind, a grievous thing!, and only evil angels will remain, who will mingle with men, and drive the poor wretches by main force into all manner of reckless crime, into wars, and robberies, and frauds, and all things hostile to the nature of the soul. Then will the earth no longer stand unshaken, and the sea will bear no ships; heaven will not support the stars in their orbits, nor will the stars pursue their constant course in heaven; all voices of the gods will of necessity be silenced and dumb; the fruits of the earth will rot; the soil will turn barren, and the very air will sicken in sullen stagnation. After this manner will old age come upon the world. Religion will be no more; all things will be disordered and awry; all good will disappear.

But when all this has befallen, Asclepius, then the Master and Father God, the first before all, the maker of that god who first came into being, will look on that which has come to pass, and will stay the disorder by the counterworking of his will, which is the good. He will call back to the right path those who have gone astray; he will cleanse the world from evil, now washing it away with water-floods, now burning it out with fiercest fire, or again expelling it by war and pestilence. And thus he will bring back his world to its former aspect, so that the Kosmos will once more be deemed worthy of worship and wondering reverence, and God, the maker and restorer of the mighty fabric, will be adored by the men of that day with unceasing hymns of praise and blessing.

Such is the new birth of the Kosmos; it is a making again of all things good, a holy and awe-striking restoration of all nature; and it is wrought in the process of time by the eternal will of God. For God's will has no beginning; it is ever the same, and as it now is, even so it has ever been, without beginning. For it is the very being of God to purpose good.

CENTURY III

CENTURY III

1   Mines are laid, some washed ashore
        the old Carib will not feel the shame
        the blame is laid at the terrorist door
        he will answer with more of the same

2   A friend in Panama, normally helpful
        changes his policy soon
        he thinks it will be to his advantage
        the rebels invade in one moon

3   When graves overflow with the young
        ones the pod and the sap are to blame
        when weapons are banned from bows to guns
        the blue hats are hunted as game

4   Throughout the world, the young in revolt
        turn language into confusion
        new ritual of dying considered a moult
        their law is non participation

5   The cure for cancer is found more certain
        using several forms of light   *Laser light used in cancer*
        the press will never give this mention   *operations. Report 4th*
        for rich, the cure as of right   *December 1992*

6   Destroying the cells shall pose no riddle
        to the man who was born in November
        destroyed in public as on a griddle
        at two and forty in a cold December

7   The Buddhist beads in a rosary
        when summed with ten times ten
        or the bricks inside an altar of fire
        tell when Typhon comes by us again

8   One hundred and twenty million feet
         to Secunderbad are walking
        the brothers soon will there entreat
        to feed the horde despairing

CENTURY III

9   From everywhere the invitation
but only one to remember
Ajita shall fly first class to Britain
to the holder of the last scepter

10   In Aza the teardrop island race
Tamils granted shelter not freedom
the government, afraid, builds new prisons
passing new laws just to fill them

The Australian 'Pacific Solution'
includes new laws and prisons
for illegal aliens. 2001 - 02

11   Bicentennial bash and joyous splurges
end in new debt failed institutions
insulted, the right will start with purges
Three year drought, then merging of nations

Retrospective. 1988 – 90
Australia

12   The collector of clocks in dark attire
through false friends will come to ruin
to teach, the left one finds desire
on Wednesday, romantic speculation.

Defeat of Labour Party, Australia.
Paul Keating

13   The false Messiah with silver hair
who would bring his country to its knees
sends the dark one to reformed Bear
both puppets are determined to please

Retrospective. Keating & others.

14   The five financiers meet in secret
to turn the loan from the Hori
the master of cooks early knows regret
silenced Peter shall paint the scenery

Maori loans swindle
New Zealand.

15   The world owes sovereignty to the New Order
each country enslaved in its debt
process completed, sunrise disorder
the last to fall in ninety eight

Universality of national
indebtedness and the fall of the
Far East stock exchanges ¢1998

16   The numbering then becomes universal
compelled in the great two of North
by the Boot found quite agreeable
the rest shall question the system's worth

CENTURY III

17   New laws passed shall number twelve
each stark in its simplicity
rules on who may fish or delve
abandoned, destroyed, the long city

18   Thou shalt not this world pollute
but recycle replant conserve
sustain, tolerate, the only route
the message shall touch every nerve

19   The grouping of the Club of Rome
Kiwi, Star, the Cape, and Aza
each shall find one spiritual home
when chaos shall bring them together

20   The red haired one whose prophet was shot   *Mormons*
by the aged dead four he is chosen
groomed for the job, by birth earns his lot
by mad war he shall lose his position

21   The mission shall be to convert the Jews
the small band turned at the border
they enter again by a different ruse
to laughter, belief in disorder

22   Those who believed in a second bible
shall come to believe in neither report
where oxen support a huge stone table
they shall build their strong new port

23   When Mercury aligns with red Mars
and Jupiter in trine conjunction
after peace, great flooding, wars
the French and the Moor opposition

24   More than a month the locusts swarm
attaining the summit of mountain
midst gales of heat, never so warm
murder, then hail, food uncertain

CENTURY III

25   After crossing the Rio Grande
       twenty years the killers advance
       when sixteen die, no help handy
       in a week, the plague found in France

26   When Vienna refuses to join the embargo
       the arms shall pour through the gate
       because of the strange and heavy cargo
       the trade in death shall abate

27   The prisoner in the armoured train
       shall draw up a new constitution
       after several years incurable pain
       then to fade to genteel destitution

28   Joint manoevers are watched from afar
       the meeting in new pandemonium
       to die from the cold the one with a scar   *Prince William*
       an end to a royal institution

29   When the cold one cannot be found
       his brother avoids the armed service   *Prince Harry*
       the buried incessant shall not sound
       Los Angels they dance like a dervish

30   In Danzig, Poznan, the workers brood
       Salidarnosc shall fight the new owner
       militancy more for rights than food
       then in Venice and London their leader

31   At a dacha close to the sea of Crimea   *Attempted coup against*
       the coup, seven the minister meet   *Gorbachev and G7conference*
       three way trade finds the third more clever   *1991.*
       to trade in diamonds, oil, and wheat

32   The avenger berserk cuts up the body
       and leaves it upon the dark strand
       his friends, aware, drink up their toddy
       the stolen gold rings on each hand

CENTURY III

33   After a fall, she her leg will lose
the husband will not see her alive
shortly his brother, credit and ruse
shall attain to the top of the hive

34   By Wills to sleep, aroused in haste
the band by the daughter is led
marches further into the white waste
holding mule and halters dark red

35   The land locked country will come to strife   *Ruanda: war between Hutus*
through tricks played one on the other   *and Tutsis. 1994 - 96*
unnecessary trouble to maintain life
when brother would shoot his own brother

36   Again the legend of the silent spring
resurrecting the Pool of Siloam
in Cymru flowers in arms as they sing
in thanks the coarse bluestone dome

37   The men of McMurdo shall leave at midnight
amid the false dawn and the fury
those in the plane will rue their plight
the grinding ice for a jury

38   Trickling streams at the glacier foot
shall swell and become a river
the shaking and the cover of soot
there is nothing that shall not quiver

39   The explosion heard in Hobart Town
shall sound like long distant thunder
the great wave washes long after the sound
causing the small ships to go under

40   Again to the summit in dawnlight wending
to worship the goddess of spring
as to Ceres and Sul each knee is bending
on each new babe, a woven ring

CENTURY III

41   To each the goddess shall assure
silent each waiting breath
old men and maidens so demure
require the rites of life not death

42   Ruin for the Russian base
the snowmen shall see disaster
everything there left in haste
never to return thereafter

43   A slow libration of the planet
two and forty degrees the measure
ninety eight years sees pluton granite
from the chasm far east of Aza

44   Eyre shall join to the sparking sea
as to north and to east it increases
then muddy flats to the south shall be
and the wildlife shall do as it pleases

45   Oysters and abalone teem
beneath the grand new bulwark
invention of the half submarine
to traverse the dark thin murk

46   Hawaii meets the same as Japan
but for fifty years a remainder
ignored at first for one lifespan
then steam and bubbles together

47   In order to carry three or four people
the craft can sink swim or fly
enclosing the crew in a plastic bubble
the meandering marshes to ply

48   The pillar shall be resurrected
and the fountain shall flow again
a woman who once defected
Miriam again is her name

CENTURY III

49   She who knew both song and dance
five times to life did return
healed but not with surgeon's lance
not all of her life work shall burn

50   Old Miriam, leader of the chosen
a longer name she was christened
to the centre of the city frozen
straight, determined, not wizened

51   Scorpio the sign of the one firstborn
picked first of a small motley lot
on an old Harley, hair windblown
long silent, at last picks her spot

52   Her scribe Venestus, the window glass
glass dragons were made by her friends
a farmhouse by the long sea grass
as from Takapuna she wends

53   After the Pole, France, and the Roman
North Africa owns the one half
Ghandi's child takes husband and pan
the crest is a lamb and a calf

54   When the city of seven is level
by quake and by water destroyed
the holy pair in direst peril
north and in terror shall ride

55   Entering the river of five mouths
she is crewed by five dead and one dying
the pestilence which passes by cows
shall leave fewer small orphans crying

56   By cholera plague and typhoid
the continent is so reduced
by hunger millions are destroyed
new strains are then deduced

CENTURY III

57   Strange mutations make a brainless beast
sometimes missing both limbs and head
the animal kingdom, great and least
shrinks to a remnant, then dead

58   The sheep are standing with vacant eye   *Reports of cataract-blinded sheep*
never nibbling the grass at their feet   *South America, Mar '92*
new diseases but no reason why   *BSE, CJD, and Foot & Mouth*
when farmers are shunned in the street   *U.K. 1999 - 2001*

59   The only survivors in the end
are those that can live in a sewer
animals whose genes mankind can bend
shall dwindle and become much fewer

60   The bottom ooze which never was stirred
takes to its belly long rivers of muck
the wrath of king Neptune so incurred
slimy deeps give new creatures suck

61   At Nova Scotia and the Scots haven
again the great orme is slain
the axolotl its closest relation
the screws shall cut them in twain

62   Poisons seeping from the coast
make tides green scum and red
the strongest men give up the ghost
eat the fish, then shortly to bed

63   The things with feathery fans reproduce
the young alive in the darkness
the legs too short are not much use
the same as was known in old Loch Ness

64   Through gossip the Canton rushes ahead
but the young girl is a betrayer
the silver lawyer who stands at the head
through secrets then shall dismay her

CENTURY III

65   A bank which stands on a busy corner   *BCCI?*
through promises false turns to fraud
the president elect turns informer
Tangiers, Bahamas, and Nord

66   Early October from leaden clouds   *Schipol Airport disaster*
the rain of sodden bright metal   *Oct 4th 1992. El Al cargo jet*
first one, another, many shrouds   *loses two engines, hits block*
lie near the southernmost capital   *of flats.*

67   The long engagement, razor sharp mind
both ended at the same instant
a run of luck seen as most unkind
the posthumous book looks like cant

68   An arrow shaped aircraft flies at three   *Columbia Shuttle*
half way around the world   *disaster, 2003*
as if frozen air, or solid wall
into tiny spread fragments curled

69   Long after the floods, Ragnarok
in year one hundred fifteen
perceived by IRAS but now a shock
again, Old Chaos shall be seen

70   Eight hundred years and ninety two
the Great Inequality cycles
Destroyer then hoves into view
bringing Old Chaos, icicles

71   Four times the size of Earth, hive
orbiting once short thousand years
Great Jove and Saturn two and five
give rise to terrified fears

72   The glassy bees shall sting in swathes
both north and south of equator
the noise and thunder shall amaze
and ten days darkness thereafter

CENTURY III

73   The largest piece falls in a wide sea
near latitude forty eight
quakes, volcanoes, then shall be
the worst not far from Torres Strait

74   In Java, Irian, Bali, Surinam
appalling wreckage and slaughter
the Barrier Reef shall act as a dam
but the Cape a disaster area

75   The crawling sheet of sparkling ice
Bhutan, Sweden, and Iceland
Denmark, Scotland, held in a vice
Canada, Sikkim, Switzerland

76   Greenland quickly uninhabited
polar bears frolic near Britain
Nepalese live in lowlands instead
New Zealand shares woes with Finland

77   Born of Typhon, the flaming star
dust and tektites bringing
Phoenix arises, with burning tar
wings of doom, skyvoice howling

78   Endless shaking shall then arise
the lord changes place with beggars
dead unburied who life despise
algal bloom, dead seas, bloody rivers

79   Unhappy confusion beyond their ken
their leader adopts a black tie
Fornier assaulted by six strong men
still dark when dawn should be nigh

80   Those in high latitudes moving south
encounter the young gangs of thugs
illiterate, radio the word of mouth
wrapped in turbans and rugs

CENTURY III

81   The fearsome toy the handheld laser
will blind but never kill
those doomed to die are left to suffer
or killed on sight or at will

82   More light than heat, the charge DIY
is punished by instant execution
In Alabama, the leader will die
sparking the organised revolution

83   Eye for an eye new meaning develops
the new shade made illegal by law
the army withdraws to the Rocky tops
destruction, snipers, men of straw

84   Book destroyers paid by computer kings
newspapers nine tenths pictures
pornography guides owned by media rings
colleges pay off their lecturers

85   Screens replace teachers in every school
subliminal input and conditioning
parents fined if kids break a rule
new prisons for both are a-building

86   Re-education for crime not punishment
school and prison mean the same
a computer invitation then is sent
the parents will be held to blame

87   CIA building transmitters of news
over-riding the TV signal
what to think & vote, kill the blues
persuading with the subliminal

88   Massive fees for megastars faces
will make the critics quite sick
the media moguls hold all the aces
they tell you whose boots to lick

CENTURY III

89   Screens are everywhere, buses, trains
       taxis, telephones, shops and planes
       the turn-off people with tired brains
       then react with bullets not names

90   The implanted strip will make you pay
       to drive your car in the city
       at only ten clicks you spend all day
       and no car will ever pass fifty

91   Defeat on the thirteenth day dawning
       interpreted according to rules
       losing by a table overturning
       reported to be a game for fools

92   The survivors group purchases wide
       in Nebraska, and South Dakota
       floods on the east side of Divide
       thirty day flood, Great Lakes area

93   April twenty-third Mississippi
       crests with Fox, Ohio, Susquehanna
       White, Arkansas, Missouri   *April 23, Davenport, 2001*
       Illinois, Allegheny, Monongahela

94   The Federal Government cannot cope
       disaster area now forty per cent
       American Red Cross loses all hope
       then money and mercy together sent

95   The Federal Reserve nearly drained dry   *Compensation, war, after W.T.C*
       Stock Market closed on Wednesday   *disaster 9/11. S/Exch closed*
       The IMF will have the mark sent high   *12th Sept 2001*
       mobs, looters, fights, by Friday

96   The bands of children roam unnoticed
       in Ohio and West Virginia
       thousands die by exposure and fist
       then desertions by the militia

Destruction of World Trade Centre, New York
9th November 2001
Verse 4:53 'Two thousand men fell jagged spires'

CENTURY III

97   Impeachment by both Houses proceeding
stalled for lack of one voice
Senate President then resigning
installs new Chiefs Arthur and Boyce

98   By reason of his incapacity
the President his office resigns
false declaration, not mutiny
recovery advanced by these signs

99   Survival Base One, first of four
contains a number of nests
each chosen man learned in lore
lies there passing the tests

100   Selected children are taught the art
of long term group survival
beginning with the horse and cart
no help from records archival

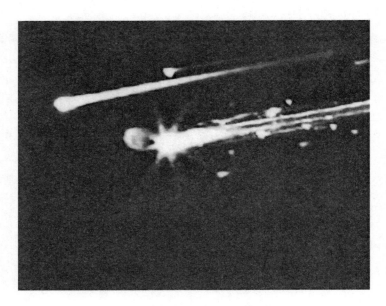

Columbia Shuttle disaster, 2003
Verse 3:68

CENTURY IV

CENTURY IV

1   Old Nos he left this century half done
     a puzzle for each commentator
     he was trying to finish it all on the run
     to get the damn thing to the printer

2   Throughout Europe the car as before
     but electric motors are king
     on three wheels, two or four,
     again one hears the nightingale sing

3   Billions spent in rebuilding cities
     the old juxtaposed with the new
     tramlines snake through street and alleys
     then the gyrotrain hoves into view

4   The single rail train is a sensation
     thinner, half open, a metal snake,
     cable towed, silent, no pylon
     one fare, one ride, by the old lake

5   By ten, wind and solar power   *UK, 2010*
     will compete with gas and coal
     atomic stations are much fewer   *Germany, Japan*
     tears for trees and short dole   *UK, dole cuts*

6   Recycling by the turn plus six
     sewage is turned to farm use
     rubbish is sorted into new mix
     new jobs are much in the news

7   When the five pound coin appears   *U.K. 27 May - 2 June 1993*
     Two currencies side by side   *Chancellor Norman Lamont*
     I promise to pay brings wry tears   *Isle of Man and British £5 coins*
     the Chancellor will not abide   *issued. Devaluation of pound.*

8   Gold and silver to nickel and brass
     turned coinage into token
     when money is burned, the upper class
     finds its power unbroken

CENTURY IV

9   Skin disorders hit all and sundry
as if chemical blight were to blame
poisons in water, air and laundry
faces hidden through eternal shame

10   Fungal sores will cover the skin
allied with cruel bacteria
to die by injection considered no sin
but done by two as a favour

11   At first the few new curiosities
who cannot live in the light
facing up to the impossibilities
underground living becomes their right

12   Named the Twentieth Century Syndrome   *Hyper-allergic children*
a revulsion for all things plastic   *and photophobia.*
living inside conditioned dome
on a diet that is not elastic

13   The Syndrome renamed the Twenty First
an explosion of the natural
no cure, no reason, if you are cursed
escape becomes more practical

14   New communities build new fences
closing their world inside
intruders shot by grim faced wenches
everything there hand-made with pride

15   The trees are treated with blown rock dust
to combat the sour acid rain
lime and granite ground in a gust
the forest shall then rise again

16   Reincarnation of the Smiling Prophet
conceived in thirty and four
born thirty five he shall not lack wit
and power upon the American shore

17   Tall and blonde where the other was fat
a Planet Planned not his message
he teaches that instinct is where it's at
updated Alistair with kind visage

69

CENTURY IV

18   Then there will come a revival of marriage
     never a vow and not in a church
     candles, dancing, flowers, no carriage
     incense, no prayer, under a branch

19   The Chinese script left to scholars
     the world will come to learn English
     decision making by predictors
     fuzzy logic by means of the squish

20   Stupidity. aggression, through DNA cured
     while secret drugs control ageing
     fear, depression, no longer endured
     new pharmacopia eases the dying

21   After the Dome in twain is riven
     a long dry spring will run
     upon the rock a new shrine arisen
     wide Ishmael wrath when this is done

22   The broken curse of years by twenty
     will yet be broken again
     eleven hundred million direct poverty
     aged sixty one, he dies in pain

23   Torn between the six point and oil
     internal dissent, no guns, no money
     lobbies will for action spoil
     over-run, the land of milk and honey

24   They will never know who pushed the button
     for the chain of command was broken
     Lanuf, Baghdad, Basra, Lebanon
     Orontes, Jerablus, Tapline

25   The river of the two lands contained
     which never overtopped its banks
     after eclipse, the dam is strained
     Egypt will not join the Arab ranks

26   P who was sent from Marseilles to Milan
     at a cost thought quite excessive
     will prove himself no flash in the pan
     a single goal proves decisive

CENTURY IV

27   After Aswan flood the drought ensues
and Tripoli invades from the west
cruelty, famine, quakes, licking dews
revolt, emigration, death for the rest

28   After revolt, the sturdy white takes
the Sudan, drives south to Equator
swings round to Chad with no mistakes
nothing held because of new saviour

29   The Ile de France and Paris deserted
through the sudden proclamation
they will hear the price demanded
the truck will terrorise the nation

30   Thank you John of Patmos Divine
for your Book of Revelation
you gave no date in any line
which caused much sad tribulation

31   Thankyou Merlin, Mother Shipton too
and the Avatars of each Age
declaiming upon your points of view
Thankyou God, let's turn the next page

32   Thankyou all the helpful dead
with messages from our relations
we think of you, sometimes in bed
in dreaming confabulations

33   Thanks be to the Ashtar Command
for warning us of our joint sins
how much true, how much yarned?
we threw it all in old dust bins

34   A line from Martin in Otahu, yes   *Martin Leo of Otahuhu, NZ,*
who adopted Leo for his name   *pacifist and poet, prosecutor*
Peace on Earth shall erupt, confess!   *in the Rainbow Warrior affair*
He wants you to know why he came   *with Colin Amery*

35   Alright Martin, of the No Zen Ashcan   *Died 1999 with a smile on*
history is by Memories Lane   *his face.*
at the end of a life's pacifist span
you will turn to the Is once again

71

CENTURY IV

36   By the age of nine they learn to live
throughout the two Americas
taking what old ones will not give
beaten, shot, cursed desperados

37   In six the spiral becomes a fright
curfew prohibits their roaming
by sewer and stealth, in half light
armoured police in the gloaming

Spiral UFO, Russia
Nepal, 2006

38   Only their leaders permitted names now
adopted from video classic
letter, number, the horde shall bow
an underclass parasitic

39   When four walls are video screens
or a maze of image telegraphic
ransom demand and British marines
at Findel and Hamburg they find it

40   Furious book savers all know the score
bad paper, ink, and pollution
nineteen hundred to second great war
two thousand great disintegration

41   The book savers will to film reduce
each and every great volume
computer terminals shall then produce
books on a screen in each room

42   The mystery long unkenned remained
a climatologist's nightmare
why the ice should advance unchained
an answer the meeting shall prepare

43   Ten names append the gloomy paper
upon wild weather, world gone mad
chaos theory will give no answer
pointing to colder weather so bad

44   After the Chicago truce is signed
they will sign the new constitution
New York separation designed
Texas, Cal, in twain are riven

72

CENTURY IV

45   Many more stars adorn the flag
from the States of Central America
through the Mex economy's sag
grasping West Indies, most of Canada

46   The Amish theme shall grow throughout
the central part of the nation
a culture dedicated to simple art
a cult becomes the new fashion

47   A membrane stretched, transparent dome   *Eden Project, UK*
shimmers to wind's deflection   *opened 2001*
beneath they shall till the sacred loam
to breathe air free of pollution

48   In England the slump and grim defiance
three hundred, sixty, and four
in shifts of six they place reliance
only one day they close the door

49   Instant print colours many and bright
demanded at touch of a button
the new machines will pleasure sight
then thrown away and forgotten

50   The unemployed will plant in rows long
the spruce, the pine, and conifer
headwaters, dumps, righting a wrong
regardless of cold, wind, and weather

51   Where a great fleet twice was wrecked   *South Korea Sea*
there they shall station a navy   *American Navy*
demanding then a great respect   *Nov, 2010*
allied, Eagle, Sun, Bear, in degree

52   A man born in Paris will subdue it
the bonnet, cane, stern visage
the Assembly dissolves, one shall rule it
then all of France, quel dommage

53   Two thousand men fell jagged spires   *Sept. 11 2001, W.T.C. disaster,*
when the Chief has eight years ended   *New York. Mayor Rudy Guiliani*
to move his seat he then desires   *elected November 1993*
against too many, his rule defended

CENTURY IV

54   Spear and shield lowered then held high
     to the sound of women grieving
     black horned man with tiger's eye
     truce, yellow flower, then fighting

55   Because of the worrying men of beer
     the Eagle and Lion, resolution
     of blue and white bringing good cheer
     to end the bloody pandemonium

56   The losses made good by Russian trade
     the opposition will be banished
     treachery, spite, tiger's tirade
     one of the first five has vanished

57   On the mountain will burn eight fires
     the Empress of Lins goes sailing
     when satisfied are all desires
     through intrigue PP shall be winning

58   The princess shall favour blue and green
     trained in law and martial art
     then in her orchard she is seen
     when her father rides a white cart

59   Princess of green, three children bears
     one cut off, two seek to rise
     fifteen, he assumes his father's cares
     ill from then, sugar to despise

60   Twelve, the Pontiff ends opposition
     law of the Church changed in degree
     for celibate priests a new decision
     women, right to choose is now free

61   The care of health comes to be rationed
     and a contribution demanded
     young interns make a plea impassioned
     then AMA splits, disbanded

62   Coming to inspect a portion of Mars
     jointly to see competition
     long perceived like outsize stars
     insufficient their resolution

CENTURY IV

63   Two shall circle the reddish globe
       entranced, and two descending
       the life within the dusty robe
       the truth they find amazing   *Life on Mars predicted*

64   A hormone which restores a memory   *February 2001*
       worth far more than weight in gold   *Viagra and Oro-Vital, the*
       inhaled the drug whose name is V   *inhaled counterpart*
       for sex mad orgies shall be sold

65   A man who cannot father children   *Viagra pill*
       can take a new pill overnight
       cancer, glaucoma, sclerosis beaten
       enkephalins relieve pain and sight

66   The sacrifices of the bloody Spring
       will be less than Autumn and Summer
       The dove of peace will then take wing
       Accord between ministers and leader

67   Low and high degree shall reach accord
       In the midst of winter discontent
       Seven days the army under a new Lord
       Poor offerings then with evil intent

68   Not all have confidence in the new Sage
       but his reputation remains untarnished
       His virtue is great in the New Age
       Adherence to the Law not diminished

69   The Sage shall enter the Temple Mount
       in dignity there he shall pray
       But he cannot bring the unity about
       Tears, cries, help, smiles, another day

70   The Sage by the Assembly, popular acclaim
       Is said to be granted the office of king
       and thus is given a different name
       meaning stability or what Heaven will bring

71   When the Dragon twice has flown by
       For a yellow star, a ship shall leave
       Adam and Eve shall the call defy
       For them, the Pacific shall upheave

72   Your maker was the fool, she said
      The Cat-god without any soul
      The king of both the stars and dead
      Wanderer from a sack of coal

73   Cat-god thing from an orange star
      Trident bearer of the Muian Deep
      Arrogant, hostile, a demander
      with eyes that can never weep

74   One day we shall learn, she said
      Mind can do more than machine
      So that when all by one are led
      Not one fleshly thing is seen

75   We have more mind than him to see
      though slant-eye has telepathy
      We have knowledge of what will be
      Our edge is our spirituality

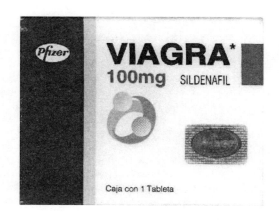

Viagra

Verse 4:64

THE CHALLENGE

"The American Administration is a bloodthirsty wild animal"
Harold Pinter, 2002

The author extends an invitation to all who doubt that the first 365 verses were written more than ten years ago, to examine and if necessary, to carbon date the original manuscript. To those who may doubt that there ever was a Miss Frances Yule who prophesied twenty years ago, her works are also open to inspection by arrangement.

To James Randi, who insists that psychic phenomena do not exist and has offered one million for proof to the contrary, we submit a set of five fulfilled verses of prophecy made by a living person. We further submit that prophecy is the queen of the psychic arts, having been practised from time immemorial to the present day.

It is further submitted that a centuries-old precedent exists to the effect that prophecies do not have to be either made or printed in chronological order.

The proof lies in the verses themselves: 1:8, 1:9, IV:53, III:95, and II:69, to be read in that order. For your convenience, these verses are now repeated as follows:

1:8	The sons, by cunning, will attain high places	a)
	The rise of the Beast advances	b)
	And starting among the northern races	c)
	a false New Order entrances	d)
1:9	Attempting to conquer all the globe	e)
	the younger knows naught but evil	f)
	Lust and greed never earned such robe	g)
	The plotting is that of the Devil	h)
IV:53	Two thousand men fell jagged spires	i)
	when the Chief eight years has ended	j)
	To move his seat he then desires	k)
	Against too many, his rule defended	l)
II:95	The Federal Reserve nearly drained dry	m)
	Stock Market closed on Wednesday	n)
	The IMF will have the mark set high	o)
	Mobs, looters, fights by Friday	p)

78

From having gained the Cowboy's ears	q)
to combat with Asia's horde	r)
Byrog counts to thirteen years	s)
For wheat, new oil is stored	t)

The following notes relate to the letters a) to t) printed on the right hand side of the foregoing verses. They are made necessary by the fact that as time passes, the details of what actually occurred are lost as web-sites are deleted and memories fade. While this booklet is destined to be forgotten, the tragic events of what has become known as 9/11 will go down ion history as the first and foremost event to mould the 21st century. It may even have been foreseen by Isaiah, whose words were: *"When the towers fall"*.

Where necessary, we provide web-site quotes and reproductions of pages that are in the public domain, for which thanks to the Google search engine which was used exclusively.

a)   Posses of lawyers disputed the recounts of votes case in the 2000 Presidential election, so that it may be said that the cunning of lawyers decided this Presidential race for 'high places'.

The sons were George W. Bush, son of ex-President George F. Bush, and Vice-President Cheyne.

b)   The Beast, which would be better put in inverted commas, may be taken to be western civilisation led by America. The Beast is characterised by its unrelenting appetite for the products of the remainder of the world; its minerals, oil, and other exports to the developed world. To this end, military, political, financial, and economic control has been refined and expanded to assure continued supplies.

c) d)   Following upon 9/11, America and the U.K. led efforts to pressure other countries into accepting the American-led 'War against terror' - the 'New Order'. It was frequently said that on 9/11 the world had changed forever, but a continuance of this 'War on terror' by means of an attack on Iraq found little support either in the West or among Arab nations, and thus the desired coalition is said to be 'false'.

e) f)   The director of Islamic global terrorism was popularly believed to be Osama bin Laden; or Osama the son of (the elder) Laden, hence 'the younger'.

g)   Bin Laden (the younger) is known to have frequented brothels and drinking establishments in Beirut which is against Islamic law, and to have made his fortune in the construction industry in Saudi Arabia. Naturally, he wears robes, not western attire.

h)   Al Qaeda, the world-wide terrorist organisation.

i)   Pictures of the 'jagged spires' are impossible to forget and require no illustration. The actual number of men on site clearing up the mess was about two thousand, with another thousand elsewhere involved in storage of steel, dumping operations, barging, administration, and support.

j)   There was only one Chief at the time, Rudy Guiliani, Mayor of New York, elected November 3rd, 1993. Thus he had nearly completed eight years at 9/11 and was present when the clean-up began.

k)   Guiliani desired to change his occupation and quit as Mayor of New York to tremendous accolades. Unsure of his future direction, in late 2002 he was making a respectable living on the lecture circuit, giving after-dinner speeches for six figure sums.

l)   There were many threats made, and some carried out, including anthrax scares, from internal and external sources that led to panic-stricken defensive measures in America.

m)   The cost to the American economy was very great, including security measures, compensation and war.

n)   Wednesday, 12th September 2001.

o)   In the new year, 2002, the German Mark would be replaced by the Euro, thus dating the prediction which cannot be later than December 31st, 2001.

p)   'Mobs, looters, fights by Friday'. Please see web-site printouts. By 'fights' the intention is obviously to infer 'fist-fights' rather than the incessant political and business 'fights' that result in very little blood being shed although plenty of people suffer thereby.

q)   The 'cowboy' is ex-President Ronald Reagan who starred in several western movies. He last spoke in person to Russian President Gorbachev ('Gorby') in 1988.

r)   War with the Taliban in Afghanistan and Russia's continuing war with the Chechens.

s)   'Byrog' is an anagram of Gorby. Thirteen years from 1988 takes us to 2001 and the war against the Taliban.

t)   Poor harvests in Russia have often meant that wheat has been imported from the West and elsewhere. 'New oil' refers to oil known to exist in several states of the former USSR but which cannot be conveniently exported. Many commentators on the American-led war in Afghanistan believed that the prime purpose of that war was to make it possible to construct a pipeline through Afghanistan to the sea. A consortium of oil companies was formed to examine the prospects which would be enhanced by a regime change in Iraq and control over the Iraq-Turkey pipeline route.

A FINAL POINT......

Assuming that the odds against a single prediction being correct are 50/50, the chances of twenty consecutive predictions are one in two to the power of twenty, i.e.:

$$1/2^{20}$$

Any reasonable person would conclude this is beyond the expectations of chance.

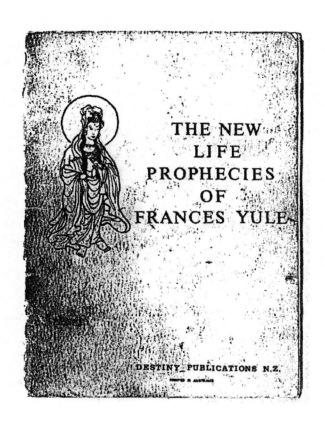

THE NEW
LIFE
PROPHECIES
OF
FRANCES YULE

DESTINY PUBLICATIONS N.Z.

PRINTED IN AUSTRALIA

A fish comes from the deep
with a message from the King of Aegis.
The sailor knocks thrice on your door
requesting permission to enter.
Give him warm hospitality and warm greetings
and he will reward you three times great.
The King of Aegis formally requests your
attendance at the forthcoming Royal Ball.
The sailor is the sign,
The fish is the emissary.
Yea or Nay, you will come -
But first the invitation proffered.

Given 1981

***

2029   The Continents have now been more or less flooded for twelve years.

2030   A prophet tries to tell the truth. People persecute each other. All World Government has collapsed.

2031   Superstition, fear and occultism run riot. Already people live on mountain-tops in most parts of the World. Many people throw sacrifices into the water to the Great God. The peak of the floods comes in this year.

2032   Hordes take to the water in boats. There are giant whirlpools, land sinks, and many are lost. All cease concerning themselves with the Prophet. The water-people seek lands to live on, and this causes much inter-racial tension between different peoples. Babies are sacrificed to the Great Water-God, Triton, for six years.

      The boat concentration is in many instances like cities - so many boats. There is murder, occultism, and every other stupid, rotten thing of which Man is capable. But in one land, Australia, life goes on as if nothing had happened, because all the sensible people are there.

However, the water is now receding, although this is not generally recognised.

2033   The land is stripped; most things being killed by salt water. The land will be re-populated as some will have had foresight to save some plants. Others will learn to live off the sea, eating seaweed and fish. The bird population will be almost entirely wiped out, but the survivors will attack humans for space in some parts, especially the Northern Hemisphere.

2034   There is no Prophet, but there is mass reorganisation among Mankind. Leaders spring up all over the World. Many people return to the land, but the population has dwindled again. About 62 million are lost in this period of reconstruction. There are many old people and not very many young people. An exodus to the salt-water lands now occurs, and also to the deserts and swamps that replace once-fertile land. The oceans are still very high.

A new science evolves, using natural sciences to make the salt-lands fertile. Humanity hates the sea, and goes berserk to clean it all up. There is insanity again. Man will dig and plant for five years, putting rotting fish in the soil, trying to break the salt down.

Men go to the mountain tops, and human chains bring down whatever soil can be found, to spread one inch deep over whatever is left. Much that is good will be learned about Earth.

2035   Another war, and a burning World. The Americans have invented a new super-weapon, throwing fireballs from a new super-napalm device.

2046   The total population of the World is now reduced to 144 million.

2047   A time again when much is achieved. There will be much psychic power, highly developed, but Man will not know how to use it although doctors tell much about the psychic sense. There is a resurgence of cetaceans and fish - great schools of them, amounting to a pestilence. We learn to speak to dolphins and whales, and start using the sea as a farming resource once again.

84

A great cache of gold is found in what was the State of Vermont. Many records are found here, causing a great depression in the spirit of the people. It takes two years for the information to go around the World. Gold now has no value as currency or a store of wealth, but is still valued as a useful metal which does not rust. All metals except iron are now in short supply.

2048   There are no leaders of any importance at this time, except for certain psychic and spiritual persons. No political system exists. A general rebuilding of the World now occurs, putting it back into shape. Man will develop high skills in the water, and some will become water-people as of necessity.

2051   Sixth Atomic war: Italy and her allies, the Italian Combined States fight Asia.

2052   The first sign of the Spiritual Leader (*born 2035. Ed.*) There are no communications anywhere; all is transmitted by word of mouth, and transport is by means of small fast semi-submarines carrying three or four people. They are built in Australia. There are still aircraft in Australia, but they are not used very much.

Australia has swung its western shore nearer to the equator, and consequently the climate has changed. This polar movement occurs over a period of over one century and is completed by 2098. The centre is now receiving more rain and is becoming green again. An inland lake has formed; an inland salt sea, which will turn the remaining eastern part of Australia into a new Garden of Eden. Millions of refugees now come to Australia, of all colours and races, inhabiting even the desert areas. The country potters along. There is still industry, but agriculture us rapidly expanding.

England has become very wet, but the climate of America remains much the same. Only about half of the World was completely flooded.

2053   Appearance (*of the Spiritual Leader. Ed.*)

2062   A big man arises, who has been fermenting 'bad juice' - a common expression of the day. His name is Joseph Demetrius Warmburg. He is a very powerful man, who owns the sub company and has been dealing with traitors. This is the man who will start it all again - the wars, the money games, and the slavery of man to overlords. In his grasp are nuclear weapons.

Many thousands of people work for him, for he is their sole source of food, the medium of exchange. Plastic money is now no longer used. From this will arise a World-wide situation, emanating from Coonabarran in New South Wales. Warmburg becomes another Antichrist type person, the power behind new politics. Australia will now claim total economic power.

2063   Germany has remained peaceful, although much of the land was flooded. The Germans have saved many essential things through foresight, and are now a gentle threat to their chief rival, Australia.

A World Council is now convened, with all the wrong people, organised by Warmburg, popularly known as Big Joe. He is a large, friendly man who will say to millions, "Let's get together." His motive is a lust for gold. He wishes to bring back money, and offers to trade food for precious metals in any form, including such things as gold pitchforks!

However, just around the corner in Australia - or Aza-aur as they call it - is a spiritual centre which recognises the danger of a system of exchange based on gold, and the despotic intentions of Big Joe. These spiritualists are psychics, able to see the future, and also powerful clairvoyants. They now convene their own World Council. The political situation will then be in reality the psychic versus instinct.

2065   Joe convenes his World Council, which is then named 'Friends of the Earth' (!) They will agree to a resumption of World Trade, together with the re-establishment of banks. Money again comes into use, called Krona. The new money resembles casino chips, with red being the highest denomination and white the lowest.

2066   There is chaos once again, because now everyone agrees with Joe, least of all the increasing number of psychics. Joe's army, based on an old unionist principle, fights a war against his own subsidiary companies.

2074	First Mass Communication.
2091	First knowledge of the Gates.
2098	Polar shift completed. New equator fully stabilised.
2104-10	Reorganisation of World Council and policy.
2118-34	Peace and rebuilding. The Prophet dies, leaving three to rule.
2129-90	The last sign and its consequences. 84 million people are now alive on Planet Earth.

***

At this point we leave a detailed history of the World to other future psychics, for the following 400-odd years is nothing but an endless succession of minor wars, tyrants, and universal chaos, comparable to the European Dark Ages, but much worse.

***

2510	China fights the Combined Hahan states.

The population of Earth has not increased, and Australia remains the only civilised country, mostly due to the efforts of spiritual leaders who have maintained order in several scattered settlements.

| 2600 | Another war is fought with weapons that are not used today. Giant cannons are built in the desert, which do not fire atomic projectiles, for all uranium is exhausted. During the last five wars of the 26th century 15 million people are lost, mostly burned to death or poisoned by radioactivity. These five wars commenced with the Chinese war of 2510. |

Humanity will have found that radioactive elements tend to concentrate in the upper waters of the sea, above the thermocline, the boundary between the topmost warm layer and the cooler bottom layer. The thermocline is now found at greater depths than used to be the case; approximately 5000 feet in some places. This has made the sea much less fertile.

Nevertheless, the necessity for obtaining food will compel Mankind to go into the less dangerous areas, where he will dig tunnels from the shore. The goal is the edible fish and seaweeds of the cold water regions.

| 2605 | Many people are nomads in the early years of the 27th century, and of these, a proportion are immature psychics, rather like the Australian aborigines. |

For transport they use a beast of burden, bred or mutated from asses. It is somewhat larger than the ass of today; distinguished by a white stripe down its back.

The politicians of the day are priests of a sort, as politics is identical with religion. There is a new Bible, collated from the writings of twelve prophets. The new Bible has a long historical section on how it came about, and why it was written. It does not contain accurate details of the Secret Millennium, but it does prophesy events up to 3035 or so.

Meher Baba will figure as a major past Avatar at this time, because of a book he had written in the 20th Century which was later discovered.

There are few men at this time, because of a fifty year succession of wars. Farming systems are quite inefficient because of a lack of large machines and the fuel to run them. Technology still exists, although it is geared more to the efficient utilisation of wind and solar power than hydro-electricity. 'Sail'[*] technology is still widely used.

There are still computers, although must advanced communication and computing technology has been lost; discarded and forgotten as useless. A continual search for lost knowledge is made necessary by a need to research the arts of survival. In many parts of the World, people have reverted to barbaric societies, struggling to survive with primitive food gathering methods.

2796   All the planets start to move on new courses. The Earth is moving further away from the Sun although the days are becoming warmer. The increasing temperature is due to a swelling of the Sun, which is more unstable than people think. The eccentricity of the Earth's orbit will increase, so that Earth will approach Jupiter before 3800.

The knowledge of this change in the Sun and the Earth's orbit results in increased efforts to find ways of leaving the Planet before it is either fried or frozen,

2803   Deroath the Beast appears.

2856-58   At this time all Earth will be aware that there is only one place seemingly under God's protection - Australia. Here is the World's spiritual centre, and also all remaining industry.

For 1000 years, Australia will be the only untouched, liveable land on Earth. Several races in Africa will therefore come to the conclusion that if there is to be any leaving of the Planet, this will be first done from Australia. They build an Ark, resembling a floating city, attempting to float there on the ocean currents. This they find possible

---

[*] (Sail technology. The motive power of the submarines first invented in the early 21st century in Australia.)

because the radio-activity in the water has decreased somewhat.

In Europe, the story is quite different, for this Continent is now covered in a plague of rats - so many that they devour everything before turning on each other.

***

2859-62 Neptune has exploded! Fireballs and meteors assail the Earth, which gains a new smaller satellite from the debris. The Moon is further away, and consequently the nights are black.

2863 The Messiah turns up! At the moment of her birth, all full psychics will know that this has happened, as she will herself. Her work among humanity will commence at the age of nine. Her name is Korana.

She will be 172 years old at the time of her greatest work, the Translation of Humanity, (called The Rapture by theologians. Ed.) All humans now live a comparatively advanced age because of life-giving plants, psychic power, and increased awareness. An age of 150 to 160 will be possible for some people.

No-one helps Korana at this time - no disciples, no prophets - no-one. Everyone does exactly as she says. All humanity has been waiting for her, because of foreknowledge and great psychic awareness.

2991 Attempts are made to build and launch spaceships in order that an old Moon-base might be inhabited again. This base consists of a large dome-type structure, and nearby is a very tall lattice tower which has a red crystal incorporated in its framework. This had been used in attempts to contact extra-terrestrials. None of the new colonists know how to use it. They are all old people, because this will not be another attempt to establish a permanent colony.

At this time, the office of Samantha is established, something like the idea of a Papess, which is held by women only. The Samanthas will be four in number, holding office consecutively. All of them will be adepts at the psychic arts, and each will be regarded by the people as both teacher and priestess.

The population of the World is still shrinking, because few children are born.

2992   The would-be Moon colonists land.   There are 2400 of them. They will never return.

Germany fights the Combined Hahan States.

2993   More spaceships leave Earth for the Moon. Three of them burn up in the atmosphere, but twenty arrive safely. They will try to grow Earth-plants.

Meanwhile, on Earth itself, nomadic people still roam, while others cull the sea, although this is not real sea-farming.

2994   A major war occurs. The subs, which are still around, are not used because this is a weapon-less war - the first of five major occult wars.

All sorts of weird things are done by means of psychic power, including the production of dragons, and the calling down of fire from the sky. For 1000 years, the World has dismissed God as such, but now Korana will tell everyone about the ultimate future of Mankind, and reveal the nature of God to the masses.

2995-99   The Prophet draws many people, organising a strong circle for the dissemination of the truth. She will have the usual Messiah-type problems!   However, this woman will convince many by some incredible miracles, including the feat of making land appear where there was none before.

3000   The year is marked by skirmishes among religious factions. Most ordinary people, those without much psychic power, are terrified. Weird cults, with weird gods, will war for even more weird motives, but there is no killing, as this will have been outlawed. Strange things are done by psychic power - walls are set up which cannot be seen, for no apparent reason. Few children are born.

New Zealand has sunk entirely.

3001   The Millennium comes, with something to celebrate. Korana, the Messiah, reveals a book containing information on the 'Gate', together with details of the manner in which it is to be constructed.   This is discovered in the Blue Mountains of Australia and it will be thought to be 2000 years old. In it we will find all secrets - all that Mankind has sought to know.

For many years, these secrets will have been partially known - available even today to those who have chosen the Paths of Enlightenment with a conviction of purpose sufficient to gain the prize.

Nevertheless, until this time Man will have never realised that mass action is required to pass the Gate, neither will he have had the leadership provided by Korana, nor the desire born of necessity for making the transit.

3031-35   An era of peace.   There are few people, no weapons whatsoever - no rockets and no guns.   Humanity has achieved the production of some very advanced tools, and the use of solar and wind power continues. At last, we, the human race, will have become sensible, striving to keep alive both ourselves and whatever else we can. Bones litter the ground everywhere, as nearly every beast has died through natural disasters and the handiwork of Man. His sole domestic beast is the water-buffalo, which although mutated to a paler colour, still bears horns and given milk. These animals will have become too valuable to eat.

***

I am the Lord!
Thy Father!
And thy Father's seed
Is held within thee.

Lo! I come again and again
And thou heedest Me not!
Wash thine hands of War
And purify thy toil.

Let us all begin anew!

Given 19 December 1980

3033   Mankind is getting ready to leave an almost unrecognisable planet, his home for millennia, Earth. This is still industry on Earth, mainly based in Australia, which is also the spiritual centre of Mankind. Ninety per cent of humanity lives on this island Continent at this time. Great changes have occurred elsewhere through the seismic events of the preceding 1000 years.

New Zealand has ceased to exist. Oceans roll where Europe used to be; a land comprised of sea and mountain peaks. Cape Horn has gone, as has the West Coast of America - left as a chain of islands inhabited only by rats. Parts of North America look like the Moon. Only blacks will live there - remnants of a once-great Nation living on a dead land.

A small part of New Guinea remains above water, while on the other side of the World, Scotland has become a series of reefs, although Ireland is still there. Half of England has gone.

Much of the land will remain green with ferns and fronds, but many of the larger trees will no longer exist. Only two species of small bird remain; a finch and a blackbird, the latter having become smaller. Even the seagulls have died out. A few penguins have also survived, although there are less than a hundred of them. In this year, the last whale dies, a strange white creature. On the land, there are no more grubs or worms in the soil, but mosquitoes have proliferated and increased three-fold in size, while harmless black beetles fly in the warmer regions - huge things like june-bugs.

The greatest natural enemy of Mankind is the rat. Billions of them have taken over all the regions deserted by Man. The day is now longer, as a World with no ice-caps slowly turns into a sterile, sandy desert.

Most small islands have gone - some collapsed, while others have been bombed out of existence. All volcanic islands have disappeared, and in the Northern Hemisphere, other volcanoes have not ceased pouring out ashes and lava. Earth is dying. Even the fish population has been reduced almost to nought, with eels and a small silvery fish like a miniature herring being the sole survivors.

3034   Earth steadily becomes more desolate, while giant farming projects proliferate, turning Earth into a long-delayed Atlantean / Aquarian reality.

In this year, the Prophet will cause an Island never before seen, to rise from the sea. She is the last of the Samanthas, called The Great Mother by many - a very powerful prophet. She will lead Mankind 'out'.

She will give the instructions for the construction of the 'gates', for they are, in reality, devices constructed by human beings. One will be situated in that part of the World once known as Britain. Another will be situated in Yass, Australia, and the third will be where the Northern Territory once was. The fourth will be upon the new island raised by herself.

The goal is Vanuta, where a Gate already exists (*See John 14:2-3*) *(See Sura 53, The Star, Koran. Ed.)*

3035   Not one fleshly living thing will be seen on Earth whatsoever.

4032   The Secret Millennium.

4061   The Completion of the Cycle.

THE LORD'S COVENANT WITH ADAM

At birth thou art at the mercy
of the creatures of your Universe -

As a child thou art at the mercy
of thine own curiosity -

As youth thou art at the mercy
of other youth -

As full-grown Man thou art at the mercy
of thine own self!

Therefore, thine life being fraught with perils
and snares fashioned in the nature of Mankind,
the Lord, thy Maker, makes the Covenant with Adam:

That, in the Kingdom of Heaven, there shall be a
Path paved, a doorway hewn, and a window set
in the door.

And a river flowing, a boat built, a wharf
constructed, so that there will be a way of
safety to the Paradise all Mankind seeks -

Paradise being the Beginning, the Now, and
the Future -
The Garden of Eden, where Man may rest in spirit
and take account of his ambition -
Whether it be as Seeker or Conqueror
(By account being equal).

Let it be known, that the Way is clearly defined,
and that any man whom the Lord deems worthy
shall walk the Walk and plough the River
as he would ask this of Me.

I was, I am, I will always Be.
All things are made of Me -
come from Me, and return to Me.

The Seeker comes of his own volition,
The Conqueror comes by My judgement.
Neither one is greater than the other.
All are equal in this Universal Creation
of Mine.

Seek the Path, and the House of God
will be known to thee.
Seek the River, and the currents will eddy
thee to the fountain's source.

This I pledge to all Mankind -
That there is no mystery
other than the mystery maker makes of his own.
Know that this is the Truth.

I am One - neither good nor evil,
Everything and everywhere.
Nothing - and vast.
Simultaneously - infinite and finite.

Therefore the Lord's Covenant with Adam
is made, and until the End,
from the Beginning to the Beginning -
As the Wheel turns its one hundred cycles.

Given January 1981

***

Note: (The Conqueror is any Prophet. The Seeker
          is any, who while not chosen, seek the Path
          to God of their own free will. Ed.)

Fulfilment of Piachi's Curious Tale

"The Acorn"

Harry Patch was, in 2009, the oldest man in Europe and the third oldest man in the world. He was a veteran of World War I and the subject of a BBC documentary *The Last Tommy*, made in 2004 and filmed at Tyne Cot, the largest British war cemetery. Here he met Charles Kuentz, one of Germany's last surviving war veterans, on September 22, the anniversary of the loss of Patch's three buddies in a lewis-gun team. A year older than Patch, Kuentz had also fought at Passchendaele, suffering a similar loss of a close friend who was killed beside him by shrapnel. Neither men had talked about his experiences until reaching his centenary.[1]

When the veterans laid a wreath together, Patch leaned from his wheelchair to pick up an acorn which he presented to Kuentz, who died a few months later. Patch died on July 25th 2009 aged 111. He said that his faith in the Church of England had been "shattered".

Back in the 1990s, a gypsy who rejoiced in the name of Piachi Diddicoy had penned a poem entitled 'Pan and the Madman' which, although fragmented, was put together by Tony Austin who published it.

Pan was the old-time god of nature, now known by the Romanies as Del, who was superseded by organised religion of many persuasions which the Romanies will use for convenience although they subscribe to none of them, much as while they accept the laws of the countries they live in, they have their own tribunals called 'kris'.

This is what Piachi wrote concerning acorns:

> A whiteleafed oak of many seasons
> Stood nearby, acorns strewed –
> Take one each, said the ancient,
> They're for the healing of the nations.
>
> Take them to the ends of Earth
> And give one to your neighbours –
> Plant them as a sign of peace,
> By that remove this Madman's curse.

---

[1] Refer also to the Daily Telegraph, 7 Nov. 2009, p.29.

Oh, how great His Light!
O Lord, O King, O Supremacy!
O wine of my unquenchable thirst -
O Vintner, red is the blood
Squeezed from Thine Own Heart,
From whence I just came,
And will, like a mad drunkard,
Return.

October 81

PAN AND THE MADMAN

Once upon a time, truth to tell,
The world of gods and men was one -
Sharing the Stars and Sun and Moon,
A sacred whole, which we call Del.

For half a million years and more,
Skin-clad men shared lions scraps -
Butchered beasts with sharp flint knaps
While gnawing upon an apple core.

Then midst Armenia's peaks and snows
Some other men came, from elsewhere -
From another place, that they held dear,
To till the soil with spade and hoes.

Half-men looked on with fear and dread,
Making noises that passed for speech -
At the Others who might even teach
How in Winter they were fat and fed.

And when grunts and yowl became word,
They asked the Others from whence they came -
How wild beasts, they could tame,
And other doings they saw and heard.

We came from the sky, the Others said,
And thence one day we shall return -
But watch! Our arts you shall learn
And our enchantments turn your head!

Years passed … the Others in a cloud
Of smoke and fire ascended on high -
Warning the folks to come not nigh,
The awful thunder grew much too loud.

So the folk thought, in a simple way
That they would now worship the Others -
So they might become their brothers
Among the stars, to which they pray.

Many years later, the story ran,
The world of gods and man was one -
A sacred whole, whose name was Pan.

Now a goatish child behorned,
Upon the twin pipes playing -
Pan was once a greater thing,
The Universe the Creator formed.

Man spoke to rocks, the sea and sky,
Saw Pan alive in wildwood growing -
Heard Pan in the wildbirds crowing,
No books were there to worship by.

Men and women with special gifts
Claimed to commune with him -
In trance-like visions, never dim,
But then the paradigm shifts…

He talks with Pan! The people cry,
Says he will intercede for us -
Our life in Heaven is now assured,
That is, if we shall ever die!

The Madman said - I have the right,
To call you when I ring this bell -
Here I have a magical string,
To lift you up to Heaven's delight!

A temple should rise with lofty span,
Build there pillars just like trees -
If you wish to hear from him,
Place a coin within *this* pan!

An old man did the 'string' untie,
With loud 'halloos' rushed outside -
A sudden idea had struck his mind,
Pan's temple was the Earth and Sky.

At once he strode back to his brethren,
Pushing aside the fuming madman -
Saying - If you believe God lives here,
I think you are mistaken!

The Immensity of Creation - he said,
Is impudently imitated here -
Your rocket-spire will not lift off,
Your nave is just a ship-full of dead!

You have forgotten the Great God Pan,
Put wooden statues in his place -
Idol worshippers to a man,
I say it is a great disgrace!

A whiteleafed oak of many seasons
Stood nearby, acorns strewed -
Take one each - said the ancient,
They're for the healing of the Nations.

Take them to the ends of Earth,
And give one to your neighbour -
Plant them as a sign of peace,
By that remove this Madman's curse.

Piachi Diddicoy

*(Note: In the Romany tongue, Del, or Devlesa,
is 'all that is above')*

Harry Patch